The Balanced Low-FODMAP Diet

Cookbook for Beginners

1500	Days Vibrant & Healthy Effortless Recipe Books Say Goodbye to IBS and Enjoy a Carefree Eating Life with 4-WEEK Meal Plan

Delcie K. Stiles

CONTENTS

INTRODUCTION I

What is the Low-FODMAP diet? I
Common Low-FODMAP Food II
What are the main food sources of high FODMAP ingredients to be aware of? II
Benefits of the Low-FODMAP Diet II
Is a Low-FODMAP Diet helpful for other conditions besides Irritable Bowel Syndrome? III
Some useful tips on Low-FODMAP IV

4-Week Meal Plan V

Measurement Conversions VII

Breakfast & Brunch 2

Thai Pumpkin Noodle Soup 2
Chicken Liver Pâté With Pepper And Sage 2
Crêpes With Cheese Sauce 3
Cheese And Herb Scones 4
Basic Smoothie Base 4
Cranberry Almond Granola 5
Overnight Peanut Butter Pumpkin Spice Oats 5
Breakfast Ratatouille With Poached Eggs 6
Strawberry Smoothie 6
Scrambled Tofu 7
Autumn Breakfast Chia Bowl 7
Tropical Smoothie 7
Hawaiian Toasted Sandwich 8
Smoothie Bowl 8
Cranberry Chocolate Chip Energy Bites 8
Potato Pancakes 9
Chia Seed Carrot Cake Pudding 9
Cheese, Ham, And Spinach Muffins 9
Cranberry Orange Scones 10
Eggs Baked In Heirloom Tomatoes 10
Overnight Banana Chocolate Oats 11
Blueberry, Kiwi, And Mint 11
Flourless Vegan Banana Peanut Butter Pancakes 11
Chocolate Scones 12
Pb&j Smoothie 12
Huevos Rancheros 13

Fish And Seafood 15

Light Tuna Casserole 15
Citrusy Swordfish Skewers 15
Grilled Cod With Fresh Basil 16
Coconut Shrimp 16
Coconut-crusted Fish With Pineapple Relish 17
Fish And Chips 17

Maple-glazed Salmon 18
Shrimp With Cherry Tomatoes 18
Atlantic Cod With Basil Walnut Sauce 19
Rita's Linguine With Clam Sauce 19
Salmon Noodle Casserole 20
Poached Salmon With Tarragon Sauce 20
Sole Meunière 21
Summery Fish Stew 21
Salmon Cakes With Fresh Dill Sauce 22
Shrimp Puttanesca With Linguine 22
Salmon With Herbs 23
Shrimp And Cheese Casserole 23
Feta Crab Cakes 24
Cornmeal-crusted Tilapia 24
Basic Baked Scallops 25
Baked Moroccan-style Halibut 25
Tilapia Piccata 26
Seafood Risotto 26
Grilled Halibut With Lemony Pesto 27
Mediterranean Flaky Fish With Vegetables 27

Meat Recipes 29

Flanken-style Beef Ribs With Quick Slaw 29
Ginger-sesame Grilled Flank Steak 29
Chicken And Rice With Peanut Sauce 30
Lamb And Vegetable Pilaf 30
Turkey And Red Pepper Burgers 31
Turkey Quinoa Meatballs With Mozzarella 31
Garden Veggie Dip Burgers 32
Fish And Potato Pie 32
Spanish Meatloaf With Garlic Mashed Potatoes 33
Mexican-style Ground Beef And Rice 33
Arroz Con Pollo With Olives, Raisins, And Pine Nuts 34
Lemon Thyme Chicken..34
Turkey Bolognese With Pasta 35
Roast Beef Tenderloin With Parmesan Crust..35
Smoky Sourdough Pizza 36
Spaghetti And Meat Sauce 36
Cumin Turkey With Fennel..37
Mild Lamb Curry...37
Red Snapper With Sweet Potato Crust And Cilantro-lime Sauce..38
Orange-ginger Salmon 38
Steamed Mussels With Saffron-infused Cream 39
Turkey Pasta With Kale 39
Zucchini Lasagna With Meat Sauce 40
Beef Rolls With Horseradish Cream...40
Pumpkin Maple Roast Chicken 41
Chinese Chicken 41

Vegetarian And Vegan 43

Quinoa-stuffed Eggplant Roulades With Feta And Mint 43
Mediterranean Noodles 43
Smoky Corn Chowder With Red Peppers..44
Mexican Risotto 44

Baked Tofu And Vegetables 45
Coconut-curry Tofu With Vegetables 45
Vegan Potato Salad, Cypriot-style 46
Mixed Grains, Seeds, And Vegetable Bowl 46
Pasta With Pesto Sauce 47
Roasted-veggie Gyros With Tzatziki Sauce 47
Crustless Spinach Quiche 48
Stuffed Zucchini Boats 48
Vegan Pad Thai 49
Collard Green Wraps With Thai Peanut Dressing 49
Peanut Butter Soba Noodles 50
Latin Quinoa-stuffed Peppers 50
Chipotle Tofu And Sweet Potato Tacos With Avocado Salsa 51
Lentil-walnut Burgers 51
Cheese Strata 52
Mac 'n' Cheeze 52
Vegan Noodles With Gingered Coconut Sauce 53
Vegetable Stir-fry 53
Vegetable And Rice Noodle Bowl 54
Watercress Zucchini Soup 54
Spanish Rice 55
Pineapple Fried Rice 55

Soups, Salads And Sides 57

Turkey-ginger Soup 57
Mussels In Chili, Bacon, And Tomato Broth 57
Chicken Noodle Soup 58
Greek Pasta Salad 58
Citrus Fennel And Mint Salad 59
Potato And Corn Chowder 59
Vegan Carrot, Leek, And Saffron Soup 60
Roasted Potato Wedges 60
Butter Lettuce Salad With Poached Egg And Bacon 61
Glorious Strawberry Salad 61
Roasted Squash And Chestnut Soup 62
Acorn Squash And Chard Soup 62
Chopped Italian Salad 63
Philly Steak Sandwich 63
Rice Paper "spring Rolls" With Satay Sauce 64
Easy Onion- And Garlic-free Chicken Stock 64
Roasted Sweet Potato Salad With Spiced Lamb And Spinach 65
Chicken Noodle Soup With Bok Choy 65
Tomato, Basil, And Olive Risotto 66
Kale And Red Bell Pepper Salad 66
Veggie Dip 67
Caprese Salad 67
Cucumber And Sesame Salad 67
Bacon Mashed Potatoes 68
Lentil Chili 68
Chicken And Dumplings Soup 69

Sauces, Dressings, And Condiments 71

Pumpkin Seed Dressing 71
Sweet Chili Garlic Sauce 71

Steakhouse Rub..71
Homemade Barbecue Sauce 72
Sun-dried Tomato Pesto 72
Bolognese Sauce..72
Ginger Sesame Salad Dressing 73
Pork Loin Rub..73
Olive Tapenade 73
Low-fodmap Spicy Ketchup 74
Low-fodmap Mayonnaise 74
Tangy Lemon Curd 75
Basil Sauce..75
Garlic-infused Oil 75
Roasted Tomato Sauce 76
Artisanal Ketchup 76
Cilantro-coconut Pesto 76
Sweet-and-sour Sauce 77
Garlic Oil 77
Sun-dried Tomato Spread..77
Basic Marinara Sauce 78
Raspberry Lemon Chia Seed Jam 78
Maple Mustard Dipping Sauce 78
Garden Pesto 79
Caesar Salad Dressing..79
Pepperonata Sauce 79

Snacks & Desserts 81

Lemon Cheesecake 81
Lamb Meatballs 82
Baked Veggie Chips 82
Low-fodmap Hummus 83
Chocolate Lava Cakes..83
Strawberry-rhubarb Crisp With Oat-pecan Topping 84
No-bake Coconut Cookie Bars 84
Lemon Tartlets 85
Cinnamon Panna Cotta With Pureed Banana..................................85
Raspberry–chia Seed Ice Pops 86
Prosciutto-wrapped Cantaloupe 86
Deviled Eggs..86
Quinoa Muffins 87
Kiwi Yogurt Freezer Bars 87
Amaretti Tiramisu 88
Cucumbers With Cottage Cheese Ranch Dip 88
Dairy-free Coffee Ice Cream..89
Layered Tahitian Lime Cheesecake..89
Coconut Rice Pudding 90
Irish Cream Delights..90
Rich White Chocolate Cake 91
Carrot Parsnip Chips 91
Flourless Chocolate Cake 92
Chinese Chicken In Lettuce Cups 92
Macadamia–chocolate Chip Cookies..93
Baked Blueberry Cheesecakes 93

Appendix : Recipes Index 94

INTRODUCTION

In the vibrant tapestry of culinary arts, few chefs embark on a mission as personal and transformative as Delcie K. Stiles. A symphony of flavors, textures, and aromas, Delcie's Low-FODMAP cookbook is more than just a collection of recipes; it's a testament to resilience, innovation, and a deep love for food.

Struggling with the unpredictability of digestive discomfort herself, Delcie recognized the profound gap in culinary resources tailored to those similarly affected. But rather than letting this challenge deter her, it fueled her creativity, leading her to curate a selection that proves dietary restrictions don't necessitate sacrificing flavor or enjoyment.

Each page of this cookbook echoes Delcie's philosophy: that food can, and should, be both medicine for the body and soul. With a perfect blend of 1500 masterfully crafted recipes and a meticulously planned 4-week meal guide, she invites you into a world where every bite is a celebration—of health, taste, and the sheer joy of eating.

As you turn these pages, you'll discover not just dishes, but stories. Stories of struggles turned into successes, of restrictions turned into opportunities, and of a chef's unwavering passion to merge healing with indulgence.

So, step into Delcie K. Stiles's culinary universe, where your gut finds its rhythm, your palate discovers new dances, and every meal tells a tale of triumph. Welcome to a transformative dining experience.

What is the Low-FODMAP diet?

The low FODMAP diet is a diet created to manage the symptoms of Irritable Bowel Syndrome (IBS) and other digestive disorders.FODMAP is an acronym that stands for "fermentable oligosaccharides, disaccharides, monosaccharides and polyols." These types of carbohydrates are difficult for some people to digest and can cause symptoms such as bloating, flatulence, stomach pain, diarrhoea and constipation. The diet consists of three phases: The Restriction Phase diet is

completely free of high FODMAP foods, usually for 3-8 weeks. The Reintroduction Phase gradually reintroduces high FODMAP foods into the diet one at a time to determine which foods trigger symptoms. The Individualisation Phase is a long-term phase in which the diet is maintained and only your specific FODMAP triggers are avoided.

Common Low-FODMAP Food

Low-FODMAP food are dietary choices designed to minimize digestive discomforts by limiting fermentable carbohydrates. Common vegetables fitting the bill include carrots, bell peppers, cucumbers, spinach, and zucchini, to name a few. When it comes to fruits, options like unripe bananas, blueberries, kiwi, and strawberries are ideal. Protein sources like beef, chicken, fish, and firm tofu remain staples. For grains, oats, quinoa, and rice are preferred, while dairy gets substituted with lactose-free versions or alternatives such as almond milk. A moderate amount of certain nuts and seeds, including almonds and macadamia, are permissible. To flavor foods, a selection of herbs and spices like basil, ginger, and thyme can be used. Typically consumed beverages in this diet range from plain water and black coffee to specific herbal teas like peppermint. It's crucial to remember that individual tolerance can vary, and guidance from a dietitian or healthcare professional is invaluable when navigating the low-FODMAP dietary landscape.

What are the main food sources of high FODMAP ingredients to be aware of?

High-FODMAP foods contain fermentable carbohydrates that can trigger digestive discomfort in sensitive individuals. Notable culprits include certain fruits like apples, pears, and peaches; vegetables such as onions, garlic, and broccoli; dairy products rich in lactose like milk, soft cheeses, and ice cream; legumes like beans, lentils, and chickpeas; wheat-based products including bread, pasta, and cereals; and sweeteners like honey, high fructose corn syrup, and sorbitol. Given the wide range of high-FODMAP foods, individuals following a low-FODMAP diet must approach these food sources with caution and ideally under the guidance of a dietary professional.

Benefits of the Low-FODMAP Diet

Symptom Relief

Many individuals with IBS (Irritable Bowel Syndrome) and other digestive disorders report significant relief from symptoms like bloating, gas, stomach pain, diarrhea, and constipation when following the diet.

Enhanced Gut Health

By reducing fermentation in the large intestine, the diet can promote a healthier gut environment, potentially benefitting overall digestive health.

Improved Quality of Life

Reduced digestive symptoms can lead to an improved quality of life, with individuals often reporting better sleep, increased energy levels, and a general feeling of well-being.

Structured Dietary Approach

The Low-FODMAP diet provides a structured approach with clear guidelines, which can make it easier for individuals to understand and manage their dietary choices.

Potential Mental and Emotional Benefits

Managing and reducing digestive symptoms can lead to decreased anxiety and stress surrounding food choices and eating in social settings.

Evidence-Based

The Low-FODMAP diet is backed by a growing body of scientific research, indicating its efficacy for many individuals with IBS and other functional gut disorders.

Is a Low-FODMAP Diet helpful for other conditions besides Irritable Bowel Syndrome?

Yes, the low-FODMAP diet, initially designed for Irritable Bowel Syndrome (IBS) management, has been researched for its potential benefits in several other conditions. Here's how it might help in contexts beyond IBS:

• Inflammatory Bowel Disease (IBD)

Some individuals with Crohn's disease or ulcerative colitis (forms of IBD) have reported relief from certain symptoms like diarrhea and bloating when adhering to a low-FODMAP diet. However, it's not a treatment for IBD itself but may alleviate some IBD-associated IBS symptoms.

• Functional Dyspepsia

This is a chronic disorder of sensation and movement in the upper digestive tract, and some research suggests that a low-FODMAP diet might help in reducing its symptoms.

Supports Informed Choices

The diet can empower individuals to make informed food choices, allowing them to navigate dining out, grocery shopping, and meal planning with greater confidence.

Comprehensive Approach

The diet doesn't just focus on exclusion but also emphasizes the importance of reintroducing foods, ensuring a balanced and varied diet in the long term.

• Fibromyalgia

Some individuals with fibromyalgia, a disorder characterized by widespread musculoskeletal pain, have reported relief from concurrent IBS-like symptoms when adhering to the low-FODMAP diet.

• Migraines

There is a hypothesis (and some preliminary research) suggesting that certain foods can trigger migraines, and a low-FODMAP diet might help in reducing their frequency in some people.

Some useful tips on Low-FODMAP

Cook at Home

Preparing your meals gives you control over ingredients, making it easier to ensure dishes are low-FODMAP.

Stay Hydrated

Drink plenty of water throughout the day, especially if you're limiting certain fruits and vegetables that might have previously contributed to your fluid intake.

Reintroduce Carefully

After the elimination phase, reintroduce high-FODMAP foods one at a time, in small amounts, to pinpoint triggers.

Diversify Your Diet

To ensure adequate nutrition, rotate through a variety of low-FODMAP foods rather than sticking to just a few favorites.

Remember It's Temporary

The strict elimination phase of the low-FODMAP diet is temporary. Many people can reintroduce several high-FODMAP foods back into their diet over time without issues.

Listen to Your Body

While the low-FODMAP diet provides guidelines, individual tolerances vary. Some might react to foods typically considered "safe" while tolerating certain "high-FODMAP" foods.

Stay Positive

Dietary changes can be challenging, but remember that the goal is improved health and well-being. Celebrate small victories and stay patient with the process.

4-Week Meal Plan

Day	Breakfast	Lunch	Dinner
1	Thai Pumpkin Noodle Soup 2	Grilled Cod With Fresh Basil 16	Vegetable Stir-fry 53
2	Crêpes With Cheese Sauce 3	Ginger-sesame Grilled Flank Steak 29	Spanish Rice 55
3	Cheese And Herb Scones 4	Mediterranean Noodles 43	Turkey-ginger Soup 57
4	Basic Smoothie Base 4	Fish And Chips 17	Chicken Noodle Soup 58
5	Strawberry Smoothie 6	Lamb And Vegetable Pilaf 30	Greek Pasta Salad 58
6	Scrambled Tofu 7	Mexican Risotto 44	Potato And Corn Chowder 59
7	Tropical Smoothie 7	Maple-glazed Salmon 18	Roasted Potato Wedges 60
8	Potato Pancakes 9	Garden Veggie Dip Burgers 32	Lemon Cheesecake 81
9	Chia Seed Carrot Cake Pudding 9	Vegan Potato Salad, Cypriot-style 46	Lamb Meatballs 82
10	Cranberry Orange Scones 10	Salmon Noodle Casserole 20	Chocolate Lava Cakes 83
11	Eggs Baked In Heirloom Tomatoes 10	Mexican-style Ground Beef And Rice 33	Lemon Tartlets 85
12	Overnight Banana Chocolate Oats 11	Pasta With Pesto Sauce 47	Chopped Italian Salad 63
13	Chocolate Scones 12	Sole Meunière 21	Veggie Dip 67
14	Pb&j Smoothie 12	Lemon Thyme Chicken 34	Caprese Salad 67

Day	Breakfast	Lunch	Dinner
15	Huevos Rancheros 13	Crustless Spinach Quiche 48	Deviled Eggs 86
16	Chicken Liver Pâté With Pepper And Sage 2	Summery Fish Stew 21	Quinoa Muffins 87
17	Cranberry Almond Granola 5	Spaghetti And Meat Sauce 36	Amaretti Tiramisu 88
18	Overnight Peanut Butter Pumpkin Spice Oats 5	Vegan Pad Thai 49	Coconut Rice Pudding 90
19	Breakfast Ratatouille With Poached Eggs 6	Salmon With Herbs 23	Irish Cream Delights 90
20	Autumn Breakfast Chia Bowl 7	Mild Lamb Curry 37	Carrot Parsnip Chips 91
21	Hawaiian Toasted Sandwich 8	Peanut Butter Soba Noodles 50	Flourless Chocolate Cake 92
22	Cranberry Chocolate Chip Energy Bites 8	Feta Crab Cakes 24	Baked Blueberry Cheesecakes 93
23	Smoothie Bowl 8	Orange-ginger Salmon 38	Tomato, Basil, And Olive Risotto 66
24	Cheese, Ham, And Spinach Muffins 9	Lentil-walnut Burgers 51	Kiwi Yogurt Freezer Bars 87
25	Blueberry, Kiwi, And Mint 11	Basic Baked Scallops 25	Prosciutto-wrapped Cantaloupe 86
26	Flourless Vegan Banana Peanut Butter Pancakes 11	Turkey Pasta With Kale 39	Chinese Chicken In Lettuce Cups 92
27	Light Tuna Casserole 15	Cheese Strata 52	Chicken Noodle Soup With Bok Choy 65
28	Coconut Shrimp 16	Mac 'n' Cheeze 52	Acorn Squash And Chard Soup 62

Measurement Conversions

BASIC KITCHEN CONVERSIONS & EQUIVALENTS

DRY MEASUREMENTS CONVERSION CHART

3 TEASPOONS = 1 TABLESPOON = 1/16 CUP

6 TEASPOONS = 2 TABLESPOONS = 1/8 CUP

12 TEASPOONS = 4 TABLESPOONS = 1/4 CUP

24 TEASPOONS = 8 TABLESPOONS = 1/2 CUP

36 TEASPOONS = 12 TABLESPOONS = 3/4 CUP

48 TEASPOONS = 16 TABLESPOONS = 1 CUP

METRIC TO US COOKING CONVERSIONS

OVEN TEMPERATURES

120 °C = 250 °F

160 °C = 320 °F

180° C = 350 °F

205 °C = 400 °F

220 °C = 425 °F

LIQUID MEASUREMENTS CONVERSION CHART

8 FLUID OUNCES = 1 CUP = 1/2 PINT = 1/4 QUART

16 FLUID OUNCES = 2 CUPS = 1 PINT = 1/2 QUART

32 FLUID OUNCES = 4 CUPS = 2 PINTS = 1 QUART= 1/4 GALLON

128 FLUID OUNCES = 16 CUPS = 8 PINTS = 4 QUARTS = 1 GALLON

BAKING IN GRAMS

1 CUP FLOUR = 140 GRAMS

1 CUP SUGAR = 150 GRAMS

1 CUP POWDERED SUGAR = 160 GRAMS

1 CUP HEAVY CREAM = 235 GRAMS

VOLUME

1 MILLILITER = 1/5 TEASPOON

5 ML = 1 TEASPOON

15 ML = 1 TABLESPOON

240 ML = 1 CUP OR 8 FLUID OUNCES

1 LITER = 34 FL. OUNCES

WEIGHT

1 GRAM = .035 OUNCES

100 GRAMS = 3.5 OUNCES

500 GRAMS = 1.1 POUNDS

1 KILOGRAM = 35 OUNCES

US TO METRIC COOKING CONVERSIONS

1/5 TSP = 1 ML

1 TSP = 5 ML

1 TBSP = 15 ML

1 FL OUNCE = 30 ML

1 CUP = 237 ML

1 PINT (2 CUPS) = 473 ML

1 QUART (4 CUPS) = .95 LITER

1 GALLON (16 CUPS) = 3.8 LITERS

1 OZ = 28 GRAMS

1 POUND = 454 GRAMS

BUTTER

1 CUP BUTTER = 2 STICKS = 8 OUNCES = 230 GRAMS = 8 TABLESPOONS

WHAT DOES 1 CUP EQUAL

1 CUP = 8 FLUID OUNCES

1 CUP = 16 TABLESPOONS

1 CUP = 48 TEASPOONS

1 CUP = 1/2 PINT

1 CUP = 1/4 QUART

1 CUP = 1/16 GALLON

1 CUP = 240 ML

BAKING PAN CONVERSIONS

1 CUP ALL-PURPOSE FLOUR = 4.5 OZ

1 CUP ROLLED OATS = 3 OZ 1 LARGE EGG = 1.7 OZ

1 CUP BUTTER = 8 OZ 1 CUP MILK = 8 OZ

1 CUP HEAVY CREAM = 8.4 OZ

1 CUP GRANULATED SUGAR = 7.1 OZ

1 CUP PACKED BROWN SUGAR = 7.75 OZ

1 CUP VEGETABLE OIL = 7.7 OZ

1 CUP UNSIFTED POWDERED SUGAR = 4.4 OZ

BAKING PAN CONVERSIONS

9-INCH ROUND CAKE PAN = 12 CUPS

10-INCH TUBE PAN =16 CUPS

11-INCH BUNDT PAN = 12 CUPS

9-INCH SPRINGFORM PAN = 10 CUPS

9 X 5 INCH LOAF PAN = 8 CUPS

9-INCH SQUARE PAN = 8 CUPS

Breakfast & Brunch

Breakfast & Brunch

Thai Pumpkin Noodle Soup

Servings:6 | Cooking Time: 55 Minutes

Ingredients:

- Roast vegetables
- 3 ¼ cups pumpkin, peeled, deseeded, and cubed
- 1 cup carrots, peeled and cubed
- 1 tsp cumin, ground
- 2 tsp olive oil
- Pinch of salt
- Pinch of pepper
- Soup
- 2 cups vegetable stock, without garlic or onion

- 1 cup spring onions, green part only, chopped finely
- 1 tsp ginger, crushed
- ½ tsp lemon zest
- 2 tsp soy sauce
- Pinch of chili flakes, to taste
- 1 ½ cups coconut milk, canned
- 1 cup thin rice noodles
- ¼ cup cilantro

Directions:

1. Preheat the oven to 350°F. Place the peeled and cubed pumpkin and carrots onto a roasting tray. Use the oil to coat the vegetables and season with cumin, salt, and pepper. Bake for 20-30 minutes, turning halfway. Remove when the vegetables are soft and golden.
2. Set the vegetables aside to cool for 10 minutes, and then blend them together with the stock until smooth.
3. Over medium heat, heat a saucepan, add some oil, and fry the spring onion for 3 minutes. Add the ginger. Let cook for another minute before adding the pumpkin and coconut milk.
4. Stir in the lemon zest, soy sauce, and chili flakes. Allow the soup to simmer for 10 minutes on low heat. Add water if the soup seems too thick.
5. Cook the noodles according to the instructions on the packet while the soup cooks. When cooked, stir the noodles into the soup with cilantro and serve.

Nutrition Info:

- 373g Calories, 16.3g Total fat, 12.3g Saturated fat, 52.6g Carbohydrates, 7.7 g Fiber, 7.4g Protein, 8.1g Sodium.

Chicken Liver Pâté With Pepper And Sage

Servings:12 | Cooking Time:x

Ingredients:

- 8 tablespoons (1 stick/113 g) salted butter, plus 3 tablespoons (45 g), melted
- 1 tablespoon garlic-infused olive oil
- 1 tablespoon olive oil
- 1 teaspoon finely chopped sage, plus more leaves for garnish

- 17 ounces (500 g) chicken livers, rinsed and trimmed (about 10 livers)
- 1 heaping tablespoon freshly ground black pepper
- ½ cup (125 ml) light cream
- Gluten-free crackers, for serving

Directions:

1. Combine the 8 tablespoons butter, garlic-infused oil, and olive oil in a medium saucepan over medium heat. Add the sage and cook for 2 to 3 minutes, stirring regularly. Add the chicken livers and cook until just browned. Remove from the heat and stir in the pepper and cream. Puree with an immersion blender or in a food processor until smooth. Add the melted butter and blend until combined.
2. Pour into six 4-ounce (125 ml) ramekins or one 3-cup (700 ml) mold and garnish with the sage leaves. Cover and refrigerate for 3 hours or until set.
3. Serve with crackers.

Nutrition Info:

- : 185 calories,8 g protein,16 g total fat,2 g carbohydrates,144 mg sodiu.

Crêpes With Cheese Sauce

Servings:4 | Cooking Time:x

Ingredients:
- CRÊPES
- ¾ cup (100 g) superfine white rice flour
- ½ cup (75 g) cornstarch
- ⅓ cup (30 g) soy flour
- ¾ teaspoon baking soda
- 2 large eggs, lightly beaten
- 1½ cups (375 ml) low-fat milk, lactose-free milk, or suitable plant-based milk
- 3 tablespoons (45 g) salted butter, melted
- Nonstick cooking spray
- CHEESE SAUCE
- 2 cups (500 ml) low-fat milk, lactose-free milk, or suitable plant-based milk
- 2 heaping tablespoons cornstarch
- 2 cups (240 g) grated reduced-fat cheddar
- Salt and freshly ground black pepper
- HAM AND SPINACH FILLING (pictured)
- Olive oil, for pan-frying
- 8 ounces (225 g) baby spinach leaves (8 cups), rinsed and dried
- 8 ounces (225 g) thinly sliced gluten-free smoked ham
- TEMPEH AND RICE FILLING
- ½ tablespoon garlic-infused olive oil
- 12 ounces (360 g) crumbled gluten-free tempeh
- ½ teaspoon smoked paprika
- Leaves from 4 thyme sprigs
- ¾ cup (140 g) cooked white rice
- 2 medium ripe tomatoes, peeled, seeded, and roughly chopped
- ½ teaspoon olive oil
- Splash of balsamic vinegar
- Salt and freshly ground black pepper to taste
- ¼ cup (40 g) pine nuts

Directions:
1. To make the crêpes, sift the rice flour, cornstarch, soy flour, and baking soda three times into a large bowl (or whisk in the bowl until well combined). Make a well in the middle, add the eggs and milk, and blend to form a smooth batter. Stir in the melted butter. Cover with plastic wrap and set aside for 20 minutes.
2. Heat a heavy-bottomed frying pan or crêpe pan over medium heat and spray well with cooking spray. Pour about ¼ cup (60 ml) batter into the warmed pan and tilt to coat the bottom thinly. Cook until bubbles start to appear, then carefully turn the crêpe over and briefly cook the other side. Transfer to a platter and cover loosely with foil to keep warm while you repeat with the remaining batter (to make 8 crêpes in total) and make the cheese sauce.
3. To make the cheese sauce, blend ¼ cup (60 ml) of the milk with the cornstarch to make a paste. Add the remaining milk, whisking well to avoid any lumps. Pour the mixture into a small saucepan and stir over medium heat until thickened. (Don't let it boil.) Add the cheddar and stir until melted. Season to taste with salt and pepper. Keep warm while you prepare the filling of your choice.
4. To make the ham and spinach filling, heat the olive oil in a large frying pan over medium heat. Add the spinach and stir to coat in the oil. Cover the pan and cook for about 1 minute, then uncover, stir, cover again, and continue to cook until just wilted, about 1 minute more. Divide the spinach evenly between the crêpes and top with the sliced ham.
5. To make the tempeh and rice filling, heat the garlic-infused oil in a large frying pan over medium-high heat. Add the crumbled tempeh, smoked paprika, and thyme and sauté until browned and crisp, about 7 minutes. Add the rice and continue to sauté until the rice is warmed through. Remove from the heat and stir in the tomatoes, olive oil, balsamic vinegar, and salt and pepper. Divide the filling evenly between the crêpes and top each with a sprinkle of pine nuts.
6. Top the crêpes with a drizzle of the cheese sauce and your choice of filling and fold to enclose. Serve with the remaining cheese sauce and a final grinding of pepper.

Nutrition Info:
- : 676 calories,36 g protein,31 g total fat,65 g carbohydrates,651 mg sodiu.

Cheese And Herb Scones

Servings:10 | Cooking Time:x

Ingredients:
- ¾ cup (175 ml) low-fat milk, lactose-free milk, or suitable plant-based milk, plus more for brushing
- 1 large egg
- ½ cup (1½ ounces/40 g) grated Parmesan
- ½ cup (2 ounces/60 g) grated cheddar
- 3 to 4 heaping tablespoons chopped herbs (such as oregano, thyme, and flat-leaf parsley)
- 1 cup (150 g) cornstarch, plus more for kneading
- 1 cup (125 g) tapioca flour
- ½ cup (45 g) soy flour
- 1 teaspoon xanthan gum or guar gum
- 2 teaspoons gluten-free baking powder
- 5 tablespoons (75 g) unsalted butter, cut into cubes, at room temperature

Directions:
1. Preheat the oven to 400°F (200°C). Line a baking sheet with parchment paper.
2. Whisk the milk and egg in a bowl. Stir in the Parmesan, cheddar, and herbs.
3. Sift the cornstarch, tapioca flour, soy flour, xanthan gum, and baking powder three times into a medium bowl (or whisk in the bowl until well combined). Rub in the butter with your fingertips until the mixture resembles fine bread crumbs. Add the milk mixture all at once and mix with a large metal spoon until the dough begins to hold together.
4. Lightly sprinkle your work surface with cornstarch. Gently bring the dough together with your hands and turn out onto the floured surface. Knead gently by pressing and then turning until the dough is just smooth (use a light touch or the scones will be tough).
5. Using a lightly floured rolling pin, roll out the dough to a thickness of 1 inch (2.5 cm) and cut out 10 to 12 scones with a 2-inch (5 cm) biscuit or cookie cutter. Use a straight-down motion to do this (if you twist the cutter, the scones will rise unevenly during baking). It's a good idea to dip the cutter in cornstarch before each cut to prevent sticking.
6. Place the scones on the sheet about ⅓ inch (1 cm) apart and brush the tops with milk. Bake for 10 to 12 minutes, until golden and cooked through. Remove the scones from the oven and immediately wrap them in a clean kitchen towel (this will help give them a soft crust). Serve warm.

Nutrition Info:
- : 179 calories,6 g protein,9 g total fat,20 g carbohydrates,172 mg sodiu.

Basic Smoothie Base

Servings:1 | Cooking Time: 3 Minutes

Ingredients:
- Base *
- 1 banana, sliced and frozen
- ¾ cup Greek yogurt
- 2 tbsp almond milk
- ¼ tsp vanilla extract
- ¼ cup ice, optional
- Flavoring variations
- Choconut *
- 1 tbsp peanut butter
- 1 tbsp cocoa powder
- Pinch of salt
- Berry *
- ½ cup strawberries, can be replaced with any other approved berry or a mixture
- 5 mint leaves
- Pinch of salt
- Tropical *
- 1 cup papaya, peeled and diced
- 1 tbsp lime juice
- Pinch of salt

Directions:
1. In a blender, add the base ingredients and one of the flavor combinations.
2. If ice is added, drink immediately or cover and put in the fridge.

Nutrition Info:
- 334g Calories, 17g Total fat, 10g Saturated fat, 36g Carbohydrates, 3 g Fiber, 9g Protein, 23g Sodium.

Cranberry Almond Granola

Servings:21 | Cooking Time:x

Ingredients:
- 1 tablespoon whole walnuts
- 1 tablespoon flaxseeds
- 3 tablespoons canola oil
- 3 tablespoons maple syrup
- 1/4 teaspoon alcohol-free vanilla extract
- 1/4 teaspoon alcohol-free almond extract
- 1 cup gluten-free rolled oats
- 1 tablespoon slivered almonds
- 1/2 teaspoon ground cinnamon
- 2 tablespoons no-sugar-added dried cranberries

Directions:
1. Preheat oven to 350°F.
2. Using a food processor or blender, add in walnuts and pulse until ground. Add to a large bowl. Next add flaxseed and pulse until finely ground. Add to same large bowl.
3. In a medium bowl, stir together oil, maple syrup, and vanilla and almond extract.
4. In large bowl, combine walnuts, flaxseed, oats, almonds, and cinnamon. Pour oil mixture over oats and stir well to combine.
5. Spread granola on a rimmed baking sheet and bake 15 minutes. Stir occasionally to ensure granola turns a light brown color.
6. After removing from oven, add cranberries and stir to combine. Store in an airtight container up to 3 weeks.

Nutrition Info:
- Calories: 499,Fat: 28g,Protein: 7g,Sodium: 6mg,Carbohydrates: 57.

Overnight Peanut Butter Pumpkin Spice Oats

Servings:2 | Cooking Time:x

Ingredients:
- 1/2 cup gluten-free rolled oats
- 1/4 cup unsweetened almond milk
- 1/4 cup pumpkin purée
- 1/2 teaspoon pumpkin pie spice
- 1/2 teaspoon alcohol-free vanilla extract
- 1/2 teaspoon ground cinnamon
- 1 tablespoon maple syrup
- 2 tablespoons peanut butter
- 2 tablespoons chopped walnuts

Directions:
1. In a medium bowl, combine oats and almond milk and stir. Add pumpkin purée, pumpkin pie spice, vanilla, cinnamon, and maple syrup. Stir.
2. Spoon half the mixture into 2 small canning jars. Add 1 tablespoon peanut butter on top of oats in each jar. Divide remaining oats on top of peanut butter. Cover with lids. Refrigerate overnight.
3. In the morning, top with walnuts and enjoy! Can be stored in refrigerator up to 3 days.

Nutrition Info:
- Calories: 270,Fat: 15g,Protein: 9g,Sodium: 92mg,Carbohydrates: 28.

Breakfast Ratatouille With Poached Eggs

Servings:4 | Cooking Time: 40 Minutes

Ingredients:

- 2 tablespoons butter
- 1 medium eggplant, diced
- 4 medium tomatoes, peeled, seeded, and diced
- 1 red bell pepper, diced
- 1 green bell pepper, diced
- 2 medium zucchini, diced
- ½ cup halved artichoke hearts
- 1 jalapeño, diced
- 2 tablespoons chopped fresh thyme
- 1 tablespoon chopped fresh oregano
- ¼ cup chopped parsley
- ½ cup homemade (onion- and garlic-free) chicken or vegetable broth
- 1 teaspoon salt
- ½ teaspoon freshly ground pepper
- 4 eggs
- 2 ounces freshly grated Parmesan cheese

Directions:

1. Heat the butter in a large skillet over medium-high heat. Add the eggplant and cook, stirring occasionally, for about 10 minutes, until the eggplant is tender. Add the tomatoes and cook for about 5 minutes, until the tomatoes have begun to break down.

2. Add the bell peppers, zucchini, artichoke hearts, jalapeño, thyme, oregano, and parsley. Stir to mix. Add the broth, salt, and pepper, and bring to a boil. Cover, reduce the heat to low, and simmer for about 20 minutes, until the liquid has evaporated and the vegetables are tender.

3. While the vegetables are cooking, poach the eggs. Bring a pan of water about 3 inches deep to a boil over high heat. Reduce the heat to low, carefully break the eggs into the water, and simmer for 4 minutes.

4. To serve, ladle the vegetable mixture into 4 serving bowls, top each with a poached egg, and sprinkle the cheese over the top. Serve hot.

Nutrition Info:

- Calories: 292; Protein: 21g; Total Fat: 15g; Saturated Fat: 7g; Carbohydrates: 24g; Fiber: 10g; Sodium: 819mg;

Strawberry Smoothie

Servings:1 | Cooking Time: 3 Minutes

Ingredients:

- ½ cup FODMAP-approved milk (almond milk is recommended)
- ⅔ cup strawberries, fresh or frozen
- ¼ cup lactose-free yogurt or vegan yogurt
- 1 ½ tsp protein powder
- 1 tsp chia seeds
- ½ tbsp maple syrup
- 1 tsp lemon juice
- ¼ tsp vanilla extract
- 6 ice cubes (only when using fresh strawberries)

Directions:

1. Cut the strawberries into halves or quarters. If using frozen strawberries, it is recommended to cut them the day before.

2. Put ingredients into a blender and blend until smooth. If the mixture gets too thick, add a small amount of hot water and continue blending.

3. It is best drunk immediately.

Nutrition Info:

- 308g Calories, 10.3g Total fat, 1.4g Saturated fat, 1.4g Carbohydrates, 5.9 g Fiber, 5.4g Protein, 30.9g Sodium.

Scrambled Tofu

Servings:1 | Cooking Time: 5 Minutes

Ingredients:
- ½ cup medium-firm tofu
- ¼ cup water
- 1 tbsp soy sauce (gluten-free)
- ¼ tsp turmeric, ground
- ½ cup grated carrot and zucchini
- Oil for greasing the pan
- 1 slice FODMAP-approved bread

Directions:
1. In a bowl, thoroughly mix together the water, soy sauce, and turmeric. Once mixed, add the vegetables and crumble the tofu into the bowl.
2. Place an oil-greased pan onto medium heat and place the mixture in it. Fry the mixture for 5 minutes or until it is golden brown.
3. Serve with a slice of FODMAP-approved toast.

Nutrition Info:
- 82g Calories, 5g Total fat, 0.5g Saturated fat, 4g Carbohydrates, 0.5 g Fiber, 5g Protein, 2g Sodium.

Autumn Breakfast Chia Bowl

Servings:2 | Cooking Time:x

Ingredients:
- 3 cups water
- 1/4 teaspoon salt
- 1 cup gluten-free steel-cut oats
- 1/2 cup lactose-free milk
- 3 tablespoons chia seeds
- 1 tablespoon halved macadamia nuts
- 1 tablespoon sliced almonds
- 1/2 teaspoon ground cinnamon
- 1 tablespoon no-sugar-added dried cranberries

Directions:
1. In a medium saucepan, bring water and salt to a boil, then add oats. Add milk and stir.
2. Add chia seeds, macadamia nuts, almonds, cinnamon, and cranberries and stir again.
3. Cover and cook 15–20 minutes, stirring occasionally until chia seeds become soft and gel-like. Serve immediately.

Nutrition Info:
- Calories: 328,Fat: 16g,Protein: 11g,Sodium: 325mg,Carbohydrates: 38.

Tropical Smoothie

Servings:1 | Cooking Time: 3 Minutes

Ingredients:
- ¾ cup frozen pineapple
- 1 cup baby spinach
- ½ tbsp lime juice
- ¾ cup ginger, ground
- ½ cup oat milk
- ½ cup coconut milk
- 1 tbsp flaxseed
- Pinch of salt

Directions:
1. Once the mixture has a smooth consistency, enjoy!

Nutrition Info:
- 434g Calories, 28g Total fat, 22g Saturated fat, 44g Carbohydrates, 7 g Fiber, 7g Protein, 20g Sodium.

Hawaiian Toasted Sandwich

Servings:1 | Cooking Time: 6 Minutes

Ingredients:
- 2 slices bread
- 1 tbsp butter
- 2 ½ tbsp pineapple chunks, drained
- 2 slices cheddar cheese
- 2 slices ham, cold cut
- 1 tbsp spring onion, tips finely chopped
- Pinch of black pepper

Directions:
1. Place a frying pan over medium heat.
2. Spread butter on the outside of each slice of bread.
3. Prepare the filling by grating the cheese, slicing the ham, rinsing the pineapple, and chopping the spring onion finely.
4. Put the sandwich together adding pepper to taste and ensuring the butter is on the outside.
5. Place in the frying pan and cook each side for 3 minutes. The bread should turn golden brown.
6. Serve warm.

Nutrition Info:
- 454g Calories, 26.5g Total fat, 9.9g Saturated fat, 33.7g Carbohydrates, 1.8 g Fiber, 19.9g Protein, 3g Sodium.

Smoothie Bowl

Servings:2 | Cooking Time: 5 Minutes

Ingredients:
- 1 cup coconut yogurt
- ½ cup coconut milk, canned or fresh
- 4 bananas, cut into slices and frozen
- 2 cups frozen mixed berries
- 2 tsp lemon juice
- ½ cup mixed nuts, chopped
- 2 mint leaves, torn

Directions:
1. In a blender, mix yogurt, milk, bananas, frozen berries, and lemon juice.
2. Pour the mix into bowls and top with nuts and mint.

Nutrition Info:
- 324g Calories, 17g Total fat, 10g Saturated fat, 36g Carbohydrates, 3 g Fiber, 9g Protein, 23g Sodium.

Cranberry Chocolate Chip Energy Bites

Servings:12 | Cooking Time: 0 Minutes

Ingredients:
- ⅓ cup oats
- ½ cup cranberries, dried
- ⅓ cup peanut butter
- ¼ cup maple syrup
- 1 tbsp quinoa, puffed
- 2 tbsp mini dark chocolate chips

Directions:
1. Mix the oats in a blender or food processor until they are a flour-like consistency. Add the cranberries, peanut butter, and maple syrup, then blend until everything sticks together.
2. Add the quinoa and chocolate and mix until everything is evenly distributed.
3. Scoop a tablespoon at a time and roll into balls. Place in an airtight container and let rest in the fridge for at least 10 minutes. Store the remainder in the fridge until eaten.
4. It can be eaten for lunch or as a snack.

Nutrition Info:
- 111g Calories, 2.5g Total fat, 1g Saturated fat, 14.5g Carbohydrates, 1.6 g Fiber, 2.5g Protein, 5.5g Sodium.

Potato Pancakes

Servings:4 | Cooking Time: 10 Minutes

Ingredients:
- 3 medium potatoes, peeled and quartered
- 2 eggs
- 2 tablespoons rice flour
- ½ teaspoon salt
- ¼ teaspoon freshly ground pepper
- 2 tablespoons coconut or grapeseed oil

Directions:
1. In a blender or food processor, pulse the potatoes until they are finely chopped.
2. In a medium bowl, whisk the eggs, and then add the flour, salt, pepper, and the finely chopped potatoes, and stir to mix well.
3. Heat the oil in a large skillet over medium-high heat. Add the potato mixture about ¼ cup at a time, using the back of a spoon or scoop to flatten into pancakes about 3 inches in diameter. Cook for 3 to 4 minutes per side, until the pancakes are golden brown and crisp. Serve hot.

Nutrition Info:
- Calories: 169; Protein: 6g; Total Fat: 3g; Saturated Fat: 2g; Carbohydrates: 30g; Fiber: 4g; Sodium: 332mg;

Chia Seed Carrot Cake Pudding

Servings:2 | Cooking Time: None

Ingredients:
- ¾ cup unsweetened rice milk
- ½ cup chopped carrots
- 3 tablespoons chia seeds, divided
- 2 tablespoons maple syrup
- ½ teaspoon vanilla
- ½ teaspoon cinnamon
- ¼ teaspoon ground ginger
- ⅛ teaspoon ground cloves
- Pinch nutmeg

Directions:
1. Place the rice milk, carrots, 2 tablespoons of the chia seeds, maple syrup, vanilla, cinnamon, ginger, cloves, and nutmeg in a blender and blend until smooth. Add the remaining tablespoon of chia seeds and pulse just to incorporate.
2. Pour the mixture into two custard cups or bowls, cover, and refrigerate overnight. Serve chilled.

Nutrition Info:
- Calories: 135; Protein: 3g; Total Fat: 5g; Saturated Fat: 0g; Carbohydrates: 26g; Fiber: 8g; Sodium: 88mg;

Cheese, Ham, And Spinach Muffins

Servings:6 | Cooking Time: 20-25 Minutes

Ingredients:
- 1 cup corn flour
- ¼ cup oats
- 2 ¼ tsp baking powder
- ½ tsp xanthan gum
- ½ cup thick Greek yogurt
- ⅔ cup lactose-free milk
- 2 large eggs
- 6 oz ham, lean
- ¼ cup chopped chives
- ½ cup cheddar cheese, grated (set 2 tbsp aside)
- ¼ cup baby spinach, chopped roughly
- ½ tsp paprika, smoked
- A drizzle of olive oil, used to grease the muffin tins

Directions:
1. Preheat the oven to 325°F and place a baking tray half-filled with water on the bottom shelf.

Cranberry Orange Scones

Servings:12 | Cooking Time:x

Ingredients:

- 3 cups gluten-free oat flour, divided
- 1 tablespoon rice milk
- 1 teaspoon white wine vinegar
- 2 tablespoons plus 1 teaspoon dried orange zest, divided
- 3/4 cup plus 1 teaspoon turbinado sugar, divided
- 1/4 teaspoon ground cinnamon
- 1/4 cup coconut flour
- 1/4 cup freshly ground flaxseeds
- 1 teaspoon gluten-free baking powder
- 1/2 teaspoon baking soda
- 1/8 teaspoon sea salt
- 1/2 cup orange juice
- 2 tablespoons unrefined coconut oil, liquefied
- 1 teaspoon pure vanilla extract
- 1/4 cup dried cranberries, chopped
- 1 large egg

Directions:

1. Preheat oven to 350°F. Line 2 baking sheets with parchment. Cover a work surface with a large square of parchment dusted with 1/2 cup oat flour.
2. Mix milk with vinegar in a small bowl.
3. In a small bowl, mix 1 teaspoon each zest and sugar. Add cinnamon.
4. In a large bowl, mix 2 cups oat flour, coconut flour, flaxseeds, remaining zest, baking powder, baking soda, and salt.
5. In a mixer, blend juice, oil, vanilla, and cranberries. Add egg and blend again. By hand, stir in milk mixture.
6. Drizzle wet ingredients over flour mixture, stirring gently. Do not overmix. Allow dough to rise and thicken, about 5 minutes.
7. Gently scoop 1/2 cup of batter onto floured workspace. With floured hands, turn dough very gently over to coat all sides. Do not knead dough. Carefully transfer flour-coated dough to a lined baking sheet and gently shape into a triangle. (Dough will spread; give it lots of height.) Repeat—adding oat flour as needed to workspace—until all dough is transferred to baking sheets and shaped into triangles.
8. Sprinkle the top of each scone with a pinch of cinnamon mixture.
9. Bake 18–20 minutes, or until tops are starting to brown. Serve warm.

Nutrition Info:

- Calories: 230,Fat: 7g,Protein: 6g,Sodium: 130mg,Carbohydrates: 39.

Eggs Baked In Heirloom Tomatoes

Servings:4 | Cooking Time:x

Ingredients:

- 4 large round heirloom tomatoes
- 3 tablespoons olive oil
- 1 teaspoon herbes de Provence
- 1/4 teaspoon salt
- 1 teaspoon freshly ground black pepper
- 4 large eggs
- 1/4 cup grated Parmesan cheese
- 1/4 cup crumbled feta cheese
- 2 teaspoons lactose-free milk

Directions:

1. Preheat oven to 375°F.
2. Slice top off tomatoes and use a paring knife or small spoon to gently remove core and seeds, making sure not to pierce bottoms of tomatoes but cutting enough flesh to leave ample space to drop in egg.
3. Arrange tomatoes so they are snug in an 8" × 8" or larger baking dish lightly greased with cooking spray. Drizzle with olive oil, and add a pinch of herbes de Provence (roughly 1/8 teaspoon each), salt, and pepper.
4. Crack an egg into each tomato. Add in 1 tablespoon each of Parmesan cheese, feta cheese, and 1/2 teaspoon each of milk.
5. Bake 20 minutes for runny eggs and 30 minutes or more for harder yolks.

Nutrition Info:

- Calories: 167,Fat: 9g,Protein: 13g,Sodium: 575mg,Carbohydrates: 8.

Overnight Banana Chocolate Oats

Servings:1 | Cooking Time:x

Ingredients:
- 1/4 cup gluten-free rolled oats
- 2 tablespoons unsweetened almond milk
- 1 teaspoon unsweetened cocoa powder
- 1/2 ripe medium banana, mashed
- 2 tablespoons lactose-free vanilla yogurt
- 1/8 teaspoon alcohol-free vanilla extract
- 2 teaspoons maple syrup
- 1/2 teaspoon ground cinnamon
- 1 ounce dark chocolate, smashed into chunks
- 1–2 banana slices, for garnish

Directions:
1. In a medium bowl, combine oats and almond milk and stir. Add cocoa powder, banana, yogurt, vanilla, maple syrup, and cinnamon; stir to combine. Place in a canning jar and cover with lid. Refrigerate overnight.
2. The next day, top with chocolate chunks and banana slices and enjoy! Can be stored in refrigerator up to 3 days.

Nutrition Info:
- Calories: 342,Fat: 11g,Protein: 7g,Sodium: 44mg,Carbohydrates: 60.

Blueberry, Kiwi, And Mint

Servings:1 | Cooking Time: 3 Minutes

Ingredients:
- 1/2 cup blueberries, frozen
- 1 kiwi, small, peeled
- 1/3 cup Greek yogurt
- 1/3 cup water
- 6 mint leaves, fresh

Directions:
1. Mix the ingredients in a blender until creamy.

Nutrition Info:
- 226g Calories, 12g Total fat, 7g Saturated fat, 27g Carbohydrates, 4 g Fiber, 6g Protein, 19g Sodium.

Flourless Vegan Banana Peanut Butter Pancakes

Servings:1 | Cooking Time:x

Ingredients:
- 2 flax eggs (see Chapter 16)
- 1/2 ripe medium banana
- 1 teaspoon chia seeds
- 1 tablespoon peanut butter
- 1 tablespoon coconut oil

Directions:
1. In a glass measuring cup, mix together flax eggs, banana, chia seeds, and peanut butter. Be sure to mash bananas well or use a blender to mix ingredients until smooth on low speed.
2. Heat oil in a medium skillet over medium heat. Pour a couple of batches of batter onto the skillet and cook pancakes until bubbly on top and golden on bottom, about 4 minutes. Flip and cook about 2 more minutes.

Nutrition Info:
- Calories: 425,Fat: 33g,Protein: 18g,Sodium: 215mg,Carbohydrates: 18.

Chocolate Scones

Servings:10 | Cooking Time:x

Ingredients:

- ⅔ cup (150 ml) low-fat milk, lactose-free milk, or suitable plant-based milk, plus more for kneading
- 1 large egg
- 1 cup (150 g) cornstarch, plus more for dusting
- 1 cup (125 g) tapioca flour
- ½ cup (45 g) soy flour
- 2 heaping tablespoons cocoa
- 1 teaspoon xanthan gum or guar gum
- 1¾ teaspoons gluten-free baking powder
- ¼ cup (55 g) superfine sugar
- 5 tablespoons (75 g) unsalted butter, cut into cubes, at room temperature
- ½ cup chocolate chips*
- Jam or butter, for serving

Directions:

1. Preheat the oven to 400°F (200°C). Line a baking sheet with parchment paper.
2. Whisk the milk and egg in a bowl.
3. Sift the cornstarch, tapioca flour, soy flour, cocoa, xanthan gum, baking powder, and sugar three times into a medium bowl (or whisk in the bowl until well combined). Rub in the butter with your fingertips until the mixture resembles fine bread crumbs. Add the chocolate chips and mix. Add the milk and egg mixture all at once and mix with a large metal spoon until the dough begins to hold together.
4. Lightly sprinkle your work surface with cornstarch. Gently bring the dough together with your hands and turn out onto the floured surface. Knead gently by pressing and then turning until the dough is just smooth (use a light touch, or the scones will be tough).
5. Using a lightly floured rolling pin, roll out the dough to a thickness of 1 inch (2.5 cm) and cut out 10 to 12 scones using a 2-inch (5 cm) biscuit or cookie cutter. Use a straight-down motion to do this (if you twist the cutter, the scones will rise unevenly during baking). It's a good idea to dip the cutter in cornstarch before each cut to prevent sticking.
6. Place the scones on the sheet about ⅓ inch (1 cm) apart and brush the tops with milk. Bake for 10 to 12 minutes, until golden and cooked through. Remove the scones from the oven and immediately wrap them in a clean kitchen towel (this will help give them a soft crust). Serve warm with jam and butter.

Nutrition Info:

- : 175 calories,3 g protein,8 g total fat,26 g carbohydrates,73 mg sodiu.

Pb&j Smoothie

Servings:2 | Cooking Time: 0 Minutes

Ingredients:

- 3 cups unsweetened almond milk
- 1 cup sliced strawberries, fresh or frozen
- 1 cup crushed ice
- ¼ cup sugar-free natural peanut butter
- 3 tablespoons chia seeds or ground flaxseed
- 1 packet stevia (optional)

Directions:

1. In a blender, combine the almond milk, strawberries, ice, peanut butter, chia seeds or flaxseed, and stevia (if using).
2. Blend until smooth.

Nutrition Info:

- Calories:328; Total Fat: 25g; Saturated Fat: 4g; Carbohydrates: 18g; Fiber: 8g; Sodium: 422mg; Protein: 12g

Huevos Rancheros

Servings:4 | Cooking Time: 20 Minutes

Ingredients:
- 8 small corn tortillas
- 1 tablespoon butter
- 4 eggs
- 2 tablespoons chopped cilantro
- FOR THE SAUCE
- 1 tablespoon olive oil
- 1 zucchini, diced
- 1 red, yellow, or green bell pepper, cored, seeded, diced
- 2 chopped jalapeños or 2 tablespoons roasted green chiles
- 2 plum tomatoes, peeled, seeded, and diced
- 1 teaspoon salt
- ½ teaspoon ground cumin
- ½ teaspoon gluten-free, onion- and garlic-free chili powder
- ½ teaspoon dried oregano
- 1 tablespoon Garlic Oil (here)

Directions:
1. Preheat the oven to 400°F.
2. Wrap the tortillas in aluminum foil and bake in the preheated oven for about 10 minutes.
3. While the tortillas are heating, make the sauce. Heat the olive oil in a large skillet over medium-high heat. Add the zucchini, bell pepper, and jalapeños. Cook, stirring frequently, until the vegetables are softened and beginning to brown, for about 5 minutes. Add the tomatoes along with the salt, cumin, chili powder, and oregano. Cook, stirring, for about another 5 minutes, until the tomatoes break down and become saucy. Stir in the Garlic Oil.
4. Heat the butter in another large skillet over medium heat. Add the eggs and fry to desired doneness.
5. To serve, arrange 2 tortillas on each of 4 serving plates, and top with a fried egg and a generous serving of sauce. Garnish with cilantro and serve immediately.

Nutrition Info:
- Calories: 257; Protein: 10g; Total Fat: 13g; Saturated Fat: 4g; Carbohydrates: 29g; Fiber: 5g; Sodium: 695mg;

Fish And Seafood

The Balanced Low-FODMAP Diet
Cookbook for Beginners

Fish And Seafood

Light Tuna Casserole

Servings:8 | Cooking Time:x

Ingredients:
- 1 tablespoon butter
- 2 large carrots, peeled and diced
- 1/4 cup gluten-free all-purpose flour
- 1 1/2 cups chicken stock
- 1 1/2 cups lactose-free milk
- 1 cup frozen green beans, thawed
- 1 teaspoon dried oregano
- 1 teaspoon dried marjoram
- 1 teaspoon dried rosemary
- 1 teaspoon dried thyme
- 1/2 teaspoon salt
- 1/4 teaspoon freshly ground black pepper
- 3 (5-ounce) cans tuna in water, drained
- 8 ounces gluten-free egg noodles, cooked al dente
- 1/2 cup shredded sharp Cheddar cheese
- 1/2 cup shredded Colby cheese
- 2 tablespoons gluten-free panko bread crumbs

Directions:
1. Preheat oven to 400°F.
2. Melt butter in a large saucepan over medium-high heat. Add carrots, and sauté 5–7 minutes, or until soft. Stir in flour and cook 1 minute.
3. Whisk in stock, then stir in milk, green beans, oregano, marjoram, rosemary, thyme, salt, pepper, and tuna. Continue cooking, stirring occasionally, about 5 minutes.
4. Add sauce mixture to noodles and toss to combine. Stir in Cheddar and Colby cheese.
5. Pour noodles into a greased 9" × 13" baking pan. Sprinkle bread crumbs on top. Bake 18–20 minutes or until top is crispy and golden and filling is bubbling. Serve immediately.

Nutrition Info:
- Calories: 339,Fat: 11g,Protein: 23g,Sodium: 650mg,Carbohydrates: 35.

Citrusy Swordfish Skewers

Servings:4 | Cooking Time:x

Ingredients:
- 2 medium oranges, peeled
- 4 (4-ounce) swordfish steaks
- 2 tablespoons Garlic-Infused Oil (see recipe in Chapter 9)
- 1 tablespoon orange juice
- 1 teaspoon dried oregano
- 1/2 teaspoon sea salt

Directions:
1. Cut each orange into six equal parts. Cut swordfish into 2" cubes.
2. Combine oil, orange juice, oregano, and salt in a medium bowl. Whisk marinade; add fish and orange pieces. Toss to coat. Marinate for 60 minutes, tossing occasionally.
3. Skewer the swordfish and orange pieces in an alternating fish/fruit pattern.
4. Heat grill or broiler to medium. Grill or broil skewers for 15 minutes, turning once, until fish is cooked through. Serve immediately.

Nutrition Info:
- Calories: 230,Fat: 11g,Protein: 23g,Sodium: 395mg,Carbohydrates: 9.

Grilled Cod With Fresh Basil

Servings:4 | Cooking Time:x

Ingredients:

- 3 tablespoons extra-virgin olive oil
- Juice of 1 medium lemon
- 2 pounds cod fillet
- 1 garlic clove, peeled, slightly smashed
- 8 tablespoons butter (1 stick)
- 2 tablespoons chopped fresh basil
- 1 pinch ground red pepper

Directions:

1. Combine oil and lemon juice in a shallow dish. Add cod and turn to coat. Marinate for 30 minutes at room temperature.
2. Heat a charcoal or gas grill to 350°F. Grill fish for 15 minutes or until cooked through, flipping once after 8 minutes.
3. When fish is on its second side, put garlic and butter in a small saucepan and cook over low heat for 5 minutes. Turn off heat, remove and discard the garlic, and add basil and ground red pepper.
4. Remove cod from grill and serve with basil sauce on the side.

Nutrition Info:

- Calories: 400,Fat: 25g,Protein: 40g,Sodium: 125mg,Carbohydrates: 1.

Coconut Shrimp

Servings:4 | Cooking Time:x

Ingredients:

- 1 slice gluten-free bread, toasted
- 1/2 cup unsweetened finely shredded coconut
- 1/8 teaspoon sea salt
- 1 large egg
- 1/8 teaspoon pure vanilla extract
- 16 large raw shrimp, peeled and deveined

Directions:

1. Preheat oven to 425°F. Line a baking sheet with foil and coat with coconut oil spray.
2. Add toast to food processor. Pulse until fine bread crumbs form.
3. In a flat dish, mix bread crumbs with coconut and salt.
4. In a small bowl, whisk together egg and vanilla.
5. Dip each shrimp into egg mixture, then into bread-crumb/coconut mixture. Transfer to baking sheet.
6. Bake for 5 minutes. Carefully turn each shrimp over and bake for 5 minutes more or until shrimp are fully cooked through. Serve immediately.

Nutrition Info:

- Calories: 88,Fat: 5g,Protein: 5g,Sodium: 160mg,Carbohydrates: 6.

Coconut-crusted Fish With Pineapple Relish

Servings:2 | Cooking Time:x

Ingredients:
- 1/2 cup shredded unsweetened coconut
- 1/2 cup gluten-free panko bread crumbs
- 1/2 teaspoon paprika
- 1 large egg
- 1 pound cod fillets
- 2 cups chopped pineapple
- 1/4 cup finely chopped red bell pepper
- 1 tablespoon fresh lemon juice
- 2 teaspoons palm sugar
- 1 finely chopped seeded jalapeño pepper
- 1/8 teaspoon salt

Directions:
1. Preheat oven to 400°F.
2. In a medium bowl, mix together coconut, bread crumbs, and paprika. In a separate small bowl whisk egg. Dredge fish fillets in egg, then coconut-panko mixture.
3. Place in a baking pan and bake 12–15 minutes or until firm.
4. Make pineapple relish by combining pineapple, bell pepper, lemon juice, sugar, and jalapeño pepper and then stirring in salt. Top fish with relish and serve.

Nutrition Info:
- Calories: 423,Fat: 11g,Protein: 46g,Sodium: 224mg,Carbohydrates: 36.

Fish And Chips

Servings:4 | Cooking Time:x

Ingredients:
- 1/4 cup millet
- 1/4 cup chopped pecans
- 2 tablespoons cornmeal
- 11/2 teaspoons sea salt, divided
- 1/8 teaspoon ground red pepper
- 4 small red potatoes, thinly sliced
- 1 tablespoon extra-virgin olive oil
- 1/2 cup lactose-free 2% milk
- 2 tablespoons light sour cream
- 12 ounces tilapia fillets

Directions:
1. In a medium bowl, cover millet with boiling water and soak for 30 minutes.
2. Preheat oven to 400°F. Line 2 baking sheets with parchment paper.
3. Drain millet completely and spread on one baking sheet. Add pecans to second baking sheet. Roast millet and pecans for 10 minutes, tossing halfway through.
4. Process pecans in a food processor until finely ground. Transfer to a medium shallow dish; toss with millet, cornmeal, 1/2 teaspoon salt, and red pepper.
5. Toss potato slices in oil and 1 teaspoon salt. Re-line one baking sheet and scatter it with potatoes. Roast in oven for 30 minutes or until brown and crisp.
6. In another shallow dish, whisk together milk and sour cream.
7. Re-line the second baking sheet and coat with cooking spray. Working with one piece at a time, dip tilapia in milk mixture and then carefully coat both sides in millet mixture. Transfer to baking sheet.
8. Bake for 15 minutes or until fish is cooked through. Serve with the potato chips.

Nutrition Info:
- Calories: 360,Fat: 12g,Protein: 24g,Sodium: 955mg,Carbohydrates: 42.

Maple-glazed Salmon

Servings:2 | Cooking Time:x

Ingredients:

- 2 tablespoons toasted sesame seeds
- 3 tablespoons maple syrup
- 3 tablespoons sesame oil
- 1/4 cup gluten-free soy sauce (tamari)
- 1/8 teaspoon freshly ground black pepper
- 1/8 teaspoon wheat-free asafetida powder
- 2 (6-ounce) wild salmon fillets
- 1 tablespoon thinly sliced fresh gingerroot
- 2 scallions, chopped, green part only

Directions:

1. To toast sesame seeds, use a small dry skillet and place over medium heat. Toast 3–5 minutes or until lightly browned, stirring occasionally. Set aside on a plate.

2. In a large, shallow dish, whisk maple syrup, sesame oil, tamari, pepper, and asafetida. Once evenly combined, add salmon to mixture and using tongs, turn fish to evenly coat every side. Place ginger slices on top of salmon. Cover and refrigerate at least 2 hours. If possible, refrigerate up to 24 hours so more of the flavors marinate throughout the fish.

3. Preheat oven to 450°F.

4. Remove salmon from refrigerator and using tongs, coat both sides of fish with toasted sesame seeds. Place salmon in a 9" × 13" baking dish and cook 10–12 minutes or until salmon is opaque in center. An instant-read thermometer should register 145°F in thickest part of fillet.

5. Transfer to plates and garnish with scallions.

Nutrition Info:

- Calories: 573,Fat: 35g,Protein: 37g,Sodium: 1,876mg,Carbohydrates: 26.

Shrimp With Cherry Tomatoes

Servings:4 | Cooking Time:x

Ingredients:

- 1 pound gluten-free spaghetti
- 2 medium zucchini, trimmed
- 1 pound carrots, peeled
- 3 tablespoons extra-virgin olive oil, divided
- 1 pint cherry tomatoes, halved
- 3 tablespoons butter
- 3 tablespoons white wine
- Juice of 1 medium lemon
- 2 tablespoons chopped fresh basil
- 2 cloves garlic, peeled and slightly crushed
- 11/2 pounds peeled and deveined shrimp
- 1/8 teaspoon sea salt
- 1/8 teaspoon freshly ground black pepper

Directions:

1. Cook spaghetti according to package directions.

2. With vegetable peeler, peel zucchini and carrots into long strips. Heat 1 tablespoon of oil in a large skillet over medium heat. Add vegetables and sauté until soft, approximately 5–8 minutes, stirring frequently. Transfer to a bowl and keep warm. Wipe the skillet clean with a paper towel.

3. In a medium skillet, combine tomatoes, butter, wine, lemon juice, and basil. Cook over low heat for 10 minutes, stirring occasionally, then keep warm.

4. While tomatoes are cooking, heat the remaining 2 tablespoons of oil in the large skillet over medium heat. Add garlic and sauté until just starting to brown, about 5 minutes. Remove garlic and add shrimp to oil. Sauté shrimp until cooked through, approximately 8 minutes, stirring frequently. Season with salt and pepper.

5. To serve, place spaghetti on a serving platter and top with vegetable mixture, shrimp, and tomato mixture.

Nutrition Info:

- Calories: 848,Fat: 24g,Protein: 52g,Sodium: 420mg,Carbohydrates: 103.

Atlantic Cod With Basil Walnut Sauce

Servings:4 | Cooking Time:x

Ingredients:

- 2 (6-ounce) Atlantic cod fillets
- 1/4 teaspoon kosher salt, divided
- 1/2 teaspoon freshly ground black pepper, divided
- Zest of 1 large lemon
- 3 tablespoons extra-virgin olive oil, divided
- 1/4 packed cup fresh basil leaves
- 1 tablespoon small walnut pieces

Directions:

1. Preheat oven to 400°F.
2. Place fish fillets in a 9″ x 13″ baking dish and sprinkle 1/8 teaspoon salt, 1/4 teaspoon pepper, and lemon zest over both sides of fish. Brush with 1 tablespoon olive oil.
3. Using a food processor, combine basil, walnuts, 1/8 teaspoon salt, and 1/4 teaspoon pepper. Process until it becomes a paste. With processor running, gradually add 2 tablespoons olive oil. Pat mixture evenly over fish.
4. Place baking dish in oven and bake for 13–17 minutes or until flesh is opaque in color. Serve with rice, spooning the juices from the pan over the fish and rice.

Nutrition Info:

- Calories: 176,Fat: 12g,Protein: 16g,Sodium: 194mg,Carbohydrates:2.

Rita's Linguine With Clam Sauce

Servings:4 | Cooking Time:x

Ingredients:

- 12 ounces gluten-free linguine
- 1 tablespoon olive oil
- 1 tablespoon garlic-infused olive oil
- 1/8 teaspoon wheat-free asafetida powder
- 2 tablespoons unsalted butter, divided
- 1/2 cup dry white wine
- 1 teaspoon dried oregano
- 2 dozen cherrystone clams, rinsed and scrubbed
- 1/4 cup coarsely chopped fresh flat-leaf parsley
- 1/2 teaspoon freshly ground black pepper

Directions:

1. Cook pasta until al dente according to package directions. Reserve 1/2 cup pasta water; drain pasta. Set aside.
2. While pasta cooks, heat oils over medium heat in a 5-quart saucepan. Add asafetida, 1 tablespoon butter, wine, and oregano and bring to a boil; cook 2 minutes.
3. Add clams; cover and simmer until clams open, about 10 minutes. If any clams have not opened, discard.
4. Add pasta to clams and stir 1 minute. Remove from heat and stir in 1 tablespoon butter, parsley, black pepper, and reserved pasta water; stir to combine. Serve immediately.

Nutrition Info:

- Calories: 456,Fat: 14g,Protein: 12g,Sodium: 14mg,Carbohydrates: 65.

Salmon Noodle Casserole

Servings:8 | Cooking Time:x

Ingredients:

- 3 small sweet potatoes
- 1 pound gluten-free egg noodles
- 1/4 cup Sweet Barbecue Sauce (see recipe in Chapter 9)
- 1 (5-ounce) can salmon, drained and flaked with a fork
- 1 cup freshly grated Parmesan cheese, divided
- 2 slices gluten-free bread, toasted
- 1/2 cup shelled pecans
- 1 teaspoon sea salt, divided
- 1/2 teaspoon freshly ground pepper, divided
- 3/4 cup lactose-free whole milk
- 1/4 cup lactose-free plain low-fat yogurt
- 1 cup Vegetable Stock (see recipe in Chapter 8)
- 1 cup shredded fontina cheese
- 1 cup packed baby spinach leaves

Directions:

1. Preheat oven to 400°F. Poke a few holes in each sweet potato and place in a small baking dish. Bake sweet potatoes for 45 minutes. Remove from oven, slice open to cool, and set aside.
2. Cook noodles according to package directions to an al dente texture.
3. Heat barbecue sauce in a small skillet over medium heat. Add salmon and sauté very carefully for about 3 minutes until fully coated. Remove from heat.
4. In a food processor, add 1/2 cup Parmesan cheese, toast, pecans, 1/2 teaspoon salt, and 1/4 teaspoon pepper. Pulse to a bread-crumb consistency. Transfer to a medium bowl.
5. Once cool enough to handle, scoop inside flesh from sweet potatoes and transfer to food processor. Add milk, yogurt, stock, and remaining salt and pepper and process to combine.
6. Add fontina and remaining 1/2 cup Parmesan cheese and pulse until combined.
7. Transfer noodles to a 13" × 9" baking dish. Pour sweet potato mixture over noodles and stir to combine.
8. Tuck spinach leaves between the noodles. Dot top of casserole evenly with salmon mixture.
9. Sprinkle top of casserole evenly with bread-crumb mixture. Bake 20 minutes, or until cheese is melted and bubbling or browning. Let sit for 5 minutes, then serve.

Nutrition Info:

- Calories: 510,Fat: 19g,Protein: 25g,Sodium: 1,140mg,Carbohydrates: 61.

Poached Salmon With Tarragon Sauce

Servings:4 | Cooking Time:x

Ingredients:

- 1/2 cup Basic Mayonnaise (see Chapter 13)
- 1/2 cup lactose-free sour cream
- 2 teaspoons chopped fresh tarragon
- 1 tablespoon chopped green onion, green part only
- 1 tablespoon lemon juice
- 1/8 teaspoon sea salt, divided
- 1 teaspoon freshly ground black pepper, divided
- 13/4 cups dry white wine
- 2 cups water
- 2-pound salmon fillet with skin

Directions:

1. In a food processor combine mayonnaise, sour cream, tarragon, onion, lemon juice, 1/16 teaspoon salt, and 1/2 teaspoon pepper; purée until smooth. (Make 1 day ahead if desired; chill and cover.) If making sauce ahead of time, allow sauce to cool to room temperature before serving.
2. In a deep 12" skillet bring water and wine to a simmer, covered.
3. Cut salmon into 4 pieces and season with 1/16 teaspoon salt and 1/2 teaspoon pepper. Submerge salmon skin-side down in pot. Make sure there is enough water to cover salmon. Simmer about 8 minutes or until just cooked through. Do not overcook fish.
4. Using a slotted spatula to drain any excess water, transfer salmon to a platter or dish to cool. Once salmon is cool, remove skin. Let salmon cool to room temperature before serving. Spoon tarragon sauce over salmon.

Nutrition Info:

- Calories: 516,Fat: 25g,Protein: 45g,Sodium: 380mg,Carbohydrates: 11.

Sole Meunière

Servings:2 | Cooking Time:x

Ingredients:

- 2 (4-ounce) boneless, skinless sole fillets
- 1/4 teaspoon kosher salt
- 1/4 teaspoon freshly ground black pepper
- 1/4 cup gluten-free all-purpose flour
- 4 tablespoons unsalted butter, divided
- 1 1/2 tablespoons finely chopped fresh flat-leaf parsley
- 1/2 teaspoon grated lemon zest
- Pulp 1/2 large lemon, seeds removed

Directions:

1. Season fillets on both sides with salt and pepper and lay on a plate. Place flour in a shallow bowl. Dredge fillets in flour, shaking off any excess.
2. Heat 2 tablespoons butter in a 12" skillet over medium-high heat. Place fillets in skillet and cook until browned on both sides and just cooked through, about 6 minutes.
3. Transfer fillets to plates; sprinkle with parsley.
4. Using a paper towel, carefully wipe skillet clean and return to heat. Add remaining butter, stir, and cook until it starts to brown. Add lemon zest and pulp; cook 3–4 minutes, then pour over fillets. Serve immediately.

Nutrition Info:

- Calories: 364,Fat: 25g,Protein: 23g,Sodium: 390mg,Carbohydrates: 12.

Summery Fish Stew

Servings:6 | Cooking Time:x

Ingredients:

- 2 slices raw bacon
- 1 cup sliced carrot
- 4 cups Seafood Stock (see recipe in Chapter 8)
- 1/2 cup dry white wine
- 1 (14.5-ounce) can fire-roasted diced tomatoes
- 1 bay leaf
- 1 teaspoon sea salt
- 1/4 teaspoon freshly ground black pepper
- 2 small red potatoes, peeled and cut into 1" pieces
- 2 pounds raw white-fleshed fish fillets, cut into 2" pieces
- 1 cup cut green beans
- 1 cup corn kernels
- 1/2 cup Whipped Cream (see recipe in Chapter 14)
- 1 tablespoon chopped fresh parsley

Directions:

1. Cook bacon in a large stockpot over medium heat. Transfer bacon to a paper towel–lined plate to cool.
2. To same pot, add carrots and sauté for 10 minutes over medium-low heat, stirring occasionally. Add stock, wine, tomatoes, bay leaf, salt, and pepper.
3. Bring just to a boil, then reduce heat and simmer for 20 minutes. Add potatoes and simmer uncovered 15 minutes. Add fish, beans, and corn; return to a simmer, stirring occasionally. Simmer uncovered 5 minutes. Remove from heat and let stand 5 minutes more, until fish is cooked through.
4. Remove and discard bay leaf. Chop and add in bacon. Stir in whipped cream.
5. Ladle stew into bowls, garnish with parsley, and serve.

Nutrition Info:

- Calories: 414,Fat: 15g,Protein: 36g,Sodium: 1,455mg,Carbohydrates: 31.

Salmon Cakes With Fresh Dill Sauce

Servings:8 | Cooking Time:x

Ingredients:

- 1 pound skinless wild-caught salmon fillet
- 3 scallions, chopped, green part only, divided
- 2 tablespoons lemon juice, divided
- 2 tablespoons Dijon mustard
- 1 teaspoon salt, divided
- 1/4 teaspoon freshly ground black pepper
- 1/4 cup gluten-free panko bread crumbs
- 1 tablespoon coconut oil
- 2 tablespoons fresh dill
- 7 ounces lactose-free sour cream

Directions:

1. In a food processor, pulse salmon, 2 scallions, 1 tablespoon lemon juice, mustard, 1/2 teaspoon salt, and pepper until coarsely chopped.
2. Mix in the bread crumbs and form into 8 patties.
3. Heat oil in a large nonstick skillet over medium heat. Cook patties until opaque throughout, about 2 minutes per side.
4. Dill sauce: In your food processor combine dill, sour cream, 1 tablespoon lemon juice, and 1/2 teaspoon salt. Pulse until blended. Dollop onto salmon cakes. Sprinkle on remaining scallions.

Nutrition Info:

- Calories: 160,Fat: 11g,Protein: 12g,Sodium: 409mg,Carbohydrates: 4.

Shrimp Puttanesca With Linguine

Servings:4 | Cooking Time:x

Ingredients:

- 1 pound gluten-free linguine
- 2 tablespoons olive oil
- 1 (24-ounce) can diced tomatoes
- 2 cups shredded kale
- 1/2 cup black olives
- 1/2 cup green olives
- 2 tablespoons capers, rinsed and drained
- 1 teaspoon red pepper flakes
- 1 pound large shrimp
- 1/2 cup crumbled feta cheese

Directions:

1. Cook pasta according to package directions. Drain and set aside.
2. Heat oil in a large skillet over medium heat. Stir in tomatoes, kale, black and green olives, capers, and red pepper flakes. Bring to a boil, then reduce heat to a simmer and cook 15 minutes.
3. Add pasta, shrimp, and cheese to sauce. Cook 3–5 minutes or until shrimp is cooked through.

Nutrition Info:

- Calories: 529,Fat: 18g,Protein: 42g,Sodium: 1,130mg,Carbohydrates: 98.

Salmon With Herbs

Servings:2 | Cooking Time:x

Ingredients:

- 1 pound salmon fillets
- 1/4 teaspoon salt
- 1/2 teaspoon freshly ground black pepper
- 1/4 cup plus 2 tablespoons olive oil
- 1/4 cup chopped fresh dill
- 2 tablespoons roughly chopped fresh rosemary
- 1/4 cup fresh flat-leaf parsley leaves
- 2 tablespoons fresh thyme leaves
- 2 tablespoons lemon juice

Directions:

1. Preheat oven to 250°F.
2. Coat a 9" × 13" casserole dish with cooking spray. Lay salmon skin-side down and sprinkle with salt and pepper.
3. Blend 1/4 cup plus 2 tablespoons olive oil with dill, rosemary, parsley, thyme, and lemon juice in a small food processor. Use a spatula or your hands to pat the herb paste over the salmon.
4. Bake 22–28 minutes depending on thickness of salmon. Insert tines of a fork into thickest part of fillet and gently pull. If fish flakes easily, it is done.
5. Slide a spatula under fish and set on a cutting board. Cut into equal pieces and serve.

Nutrition Info:

- Calories: 588,Fat: 44g,Protein: 45g,Sodium: 403mg,Carbohydrates: 3.

Shrimp And Cheese Casserole

Servings:4 | Cooking Time:x

Ingredients:

- 3 tablespoons butter
- 1/8 teaspoon salt
- 1/8 teaspoon freshly ground black pepper
- 1/8 teaspoon wheat-free asafetida powder
- 1/4 cup dry white wine
- 10 ounces fresh spinach, chopped
- 1 (14.5-ounce) can diced tomatoes, drained
- 10 ounces medium shrimp, peeled and deveined
- 2 tablespoons olive oil
- 1/4 pound crumbled feta cheese
- 1/4 pound shredded mozzarella cheese

Directions:

1. Preheat oven to 350°F. Grease a 9" × 13"casserole dish.
2. In a large skillet, melt butter over medium-high heat; add salt, pepper, and asafetida and stir.
3. Add wine and spinach and cook 2–3 minutes.
4. Put spinach mixture into prepared casserole dish and layer in diced tomatoes. Place shrimp on top, drizzle with olive oil. Sprinkle with feta and mozzarella.
5. Bake 25 minutes or until cheese is bubbly and slightly brown.

Nutrition Info:

- Calories: 346,Fat: 22g,Protein: 27g,Sodium: 790mg,Carbohydrates: 8.

Feta Crab Cakes

Servings:4 | Cooking Time:x

Ingredients:

- 5 slices gluten-free bread, toasted
- 1/2 teaspoon sea salt
- 1/8 teaspoon freshly ground black pepper
- 12 ounces lump cooked crabmeat
- 1/2 cup crumbled feta cheese
- 1/2 teaspoon dried basil
- 1/2 teaspoon dried oregano
- 1/2 teaspoon dried marjoram
- 1/2 teaspoon dried thyme
- 1 tablespoon lactose-free plain low-fat yogurt
- 1 large egg, beaten, divided

Directions:

1. Preheat oven to 400°F. Line a baking sheet with parchment paper and brush with safflower oil.
2. Add toast, salt, and pepper to a food processor. Pulse until fine bread crumbs form.
3. In a large bowl, combine 1/3 cup bread crumbs, crabmeat, feta, basil, oregano, marjoram, thyme, yogurt, and 1 tablespoon beaten egg. Stir well to combine.
4. Place remaining beaten egg in a bowl. Place remaining bread crumbs in a separate shallow bowl. Create 8 equal round balls of crab mixture. Working with one ball at a time, flatten to a 1/2" disc, then coat in egg, followed by bread crumbs. Transfer to baking sheet.
5. Bake 10 minutes, then carefully turn each cake over and bake 10 minutes more.

Nutrition Info:

- Calories: 270,Fat: 7g,Protein: 26g,Sodium: 1,065mg,Carbohydrates: 24.

Cornmeal-crusted Tilapia

Servings:2 | Cooking Time:x

Ingredients:

- 1 pound tilapia
- 1/4 cup gluten-free bread crumbs
- 3/4 cup coarse cornmeal
- 2 tablespoons gluten-free all-purpose flour
- 1/2 teaspoon salt
- 1 teaspoon freshly ground black pepper
- 1/8 teaspoon wheat-free asafetida powder
- 1 large egg
- 1 tablespoon lactose-free milk
- 1 tablespoon sunflower oil

Directions:

1. Rinse and pat fish dry. Slice into 2 pieces.
2. In a large bowl, combine bread crumbs, cornmeal, flour, salt, pepper, and asafetida. In a small bowl, whisk together egg and milk.
3. Dip tilapia in egg mixture, tapping off any excess. Then dip both sides of fish in cornmeal mixture.
4. Heat oil in a 9" frying pan on medium-high heat. Pan-fry fish 3–5 minutes each side; fish should be opaque throughout and flaky.

Nutrition Info:

- Calories: 561,Fat: 13g,Protein: 50g,Sodium: 882mg,Carbohydrates: 58.

Basic Baked Scallops

Servings:2 | Cooking Time:x

Ingredients:
- 3⁄4 pound sea scallops
- 2 tablespoons lemon juice
- 2 1⁄2 tablespoons unsalted butter, melted
- 1⁄4 teaspoon sea salt
- 1⁄2 teaspoon freshly ground black pepper
- 2 tablespoons chopped fresh flat-leaf parsley
- 1⁄2 cup gluten-free bread crumbs
- 1⁄2 teaspoon smoked paprika
- 2 tablespoons olive oil

Directions:
1. Preheat oven to 425°F.
2. Toss together scallops, lemon juice, melted butter, salt, and pepper in a 2-quart baking dish.
3. In a medium bowl, combine parsley, bread crumbs, paprika, and olive oil. Sprinkle on top of scallops.
4. Bake 12–14 minutes or until scallops are heated through and bread crumbs are golden. Serve immediately.

Nutrition Info:
- Calories: 426,Fat: 30g,Protein: 17g,Sodium: 621mg,Carbohydrates: 23.

Baked Moroccan-style Halibut

Servings:4 | Cooking Time:x

Ingredients:
- 1 pint cherry tomatoes
- 1⁄4 cup pitted black olives
- 1⁄8 teaspoon wheat-free asafetida powder
- 1⁄2 teaspoon ground cumin
- 1⁄4 teaspoon ground cinnamon
- 1⁄4 teaspoon freshly ground black pepper
- 4 (6-ounce) fresh halibut fillets
- 2 tablespoons olive oil

Directions:
1. Preheat oven 450°F.
2. In a medium mixing bowl, stir together tomatoes, olives, asafetida, cumin, cinnamon, and black pepper.
3. Add halibut to a large baking dish. Sprinkle tomato mixture evenly over fish. Drizzle oil over fish.
4. Bake 10–15 minutes or until an instant-read thermometer inserted into the thickest fillet reads 145°F. Serve immediately.

Nutrition Info:
- Calories: 269,Fat: 12g,Protein: 36g,Sodium: 168mg,Carbohydrates: 4.

Tilapia Piccata

Servings:6 | Cooking Time:x

Ingredients:

- 1⁄4 cup dry white wine
- 3 tablespoons freshly squeezed lemon juice, preferably Meyer
- 1 teaspoon fresh lemon zest
- 2 tablespoons capers, rinsed, drained
- 1⁄4 cup sweet rice flour, divided
- 1⁄2 teaspoon sea salt
- 1⁄4 teaspoon freshly ground black pepper
- 4 (6-ounce) pieces tilapia fillets
- 1 tablespoon Garlic-Infused Oil (see recipe in Chapter 9)
- 1 teaspoon butter
- 1 tablespoon chopped fresh parsley

Directions:

1. In a small bowl, whisk wine, lemon juice, zest, and capers.
2. Reserve 1 teaspoon flour and set aside. Mix remaining flour with salt and pepper on a plate. Dip fish into flour.
3. Heat oil over medium heat in a large skillet. Add fish and cook 2–3 minutes per side. When fish is cooked through, remove from pan.
4. Add wine mixture and reserved flour to pan and cook 1 minute, whisking constantly. Remove from heat and stir in butter.
5. Top fish with the sauce, garnish with parsley, and serve immediately.

Nutrition Info:

- Calories: 168,Fat: 5g,Protein: 23g,Sodium: 342mg,Carbohydrates: 6.

Seafood Risotto

Servings:6 | Cooking Time:x

Ingredients:

- 21⁄2 cups water
- 2 (8-ounce) bottles clam juice
- 6 tablespoons olive oil, divided
- 11⁄2 cups arborio rice
- 1⁄2 cup dry white wine
- 3⁄4 pound uncooked large shrimp, peeled, deveined,
- coarsely chopped
- 3⁄4 pound bay scallops
- 1⁄8 teaspoon wheat-free asafetida powder
- 1 tablespoon butter
- 1⁄2 cup grated Parmesan cheese
- 2 tablespoons finely chopped fresh Italian parsley

Directions:

1. Combine water and clam juice in a medium saucepan. Bring to simmer. Keep warm over low heat.
2. Heat 3 tablespoons oil in heavy, large saucepan over medium heat. Add rice; sauté 2 minutes.
3. Add wine; stir until liquid is absorbed, about 2 minutes. Add 1 cup clam juice mixture to rice. Simmer until liquid is absorbed, stirring often. Continue adding clam juice mixture 1⁄2 cup at a time, stirring often and simmering until liquid is absorbed before each addition. Simmer until rice is tender but still slightly firm in center and mixture is creamy, about 25 minutes.
4. Heat remaining 3 tablespoons oil in a separate heavy, large skillet over medium-high heat. Add shrimp, scallops, and asafetida. Sauté until shrimp and scallops are opaque in center, about 6 minutes.
5. Add seafood to rice. Stir and add butter; cook 4 minutes longer. Remove from heat and stir in Parmesan cheese. Transfer to serving bowl.
6. Garnish with chopped parsley and serve.

Nutrition Info:

- Calories: 514,Fat: 22g,Protein: 30g,Sodium: 478mg,Carbohydrates: 43.

Grilled Halibut With Lemony Pesto

Servings:4 | Cooking Time:x

Ingredients:

- 1 tablespoon grapeseed oil
- 2 tablespoons freshly squeezed lemon juice, divided
- 2 teaspoons grated lemon zest, divided
- 1/2 teaspoon sea salt
- 1/4 teaspoon freshly ground black pepper
- 4 (6-ounce) raw halibut steaks
- 1/2 cup Garden Pesto (see recipe in Chapter 9)

Directions:

1. Whisk oil, 1 tablespoon lemon juice, 1 teaspoon zest, salt, and pepper in a large bowl. Add halibut and marinate for 30 minutes.
2. Add pesto, remaining juice, and remaining zest to a food processor. Pulse just until combined.
3. Heat a charcoal grill, gas grill, or broiler to 350°F. Grill or broil steaks, about 6 minutes per side until fish is cooked through.
4. Top fish with the lemony pesto and serve immediately.

Nutrition Info:

- Calories: 356,Fat: 20g,Protein: 39g,Sodium: 675mg,Carbohydrates: 3.

Mediterranean Flaky Fish With Vegetables

Servings:4 | Cooking Time:x

Ingredients:

- 4 (3.5-ounce) skinless Atlantic cod fillets
- 1 cup grated zucchini
- 1/4 cup thinly sliced fresh basil, plus 4 whole basil leaves
- 20 cherry tomatoes, halved
- 10 black olives, sliced
- 1/4 teaspoon kosher salt
- 1/2 teaspoon freshly ground black pepper
- 4 tablespoons dry white wine, divided
- 4 tablespoons extra-virgin olive oil, divided

Directions:

1. Preheat oven to 400°F.
2. Make parchment pockets: Pull out a 17" × 11" piece of parchment paper. With one longer edge closest to you, fold in half from left to right. Using scissors, cut out a large heart shape. On a large cutting board or clean work surface, lay down parchment heart and place fish on one half of heart, leaving at least a 11/2" border around fillet. Repeat with remaining fish fillets. Lay parchment hearts in a 9" × 13" baking dish.
3. In a medium bowl, combine zucchini, sliced basil, tomatoes, olives, salt, and pepper. Stir to combine.
4. Evenly distribute the vegetables over each fish fillet in the parchment hearts.
5. Take opposite side of each parchment heart and fold over, making both edges of heart line up. Starting at rounded end, crimp edges together tightly. Leave a few inches at pointed end unfolded. Grab pointed edge and tilt heart to pour in 1 tablespoon each of wine and oil. Finish by crimping edges and twisting pointed end around and under packet.
6. Bake until just cooked through, about 10–12 minutes. Poke a toothpick through parchment paper. Fish should be done if toothpick easily slides through fish. Carefully cut open packets (steam will escape). Garnish with whole basil leaves.

Nutrition Info:

- Calories: 246,Fat: 16g,Protein: 19g,Sodium: 304mg,Carbohydrates: 6.

Meat Recipes

The Balanced Low-FODMAP Diet
Cookbook for Beginners

Meat Recipes

Flanken-style Beef Ribs With Quick Slaw

Servings:4 | Cooking Time: 8 Minutes

Ingredients:

- 1 pound flanken-style beef ribs
- ½ teaspoon sea salt
- ⅛ teaspoon freshly ground black pepper
- 2 tablespoons Garlic Oil
- 2 cups shredded cabbage
- 6 scallions, green parts only, chopped
- ¼ cup Lemon-Dill Vinaigrette

Directions:

1. Season the ribs with salt and pepper.
2. In a large nonstick skillet over medium-high heat, heat the garlic oil until it shimmers.
3. Add the ribs and cook for about 4 minutes per side, or until browned.
4. In a large bowl, combine the cabbage, scallions, and vinaigrette. Toss to combine.

Nutrition Info:

- Calories:357; Total Fat: 22g; Saturated Fat: 5; Carbohydrates: 4g; Fiber: 2g; Sodium: 319mg; Protein: 35g

Ginger-sesame Grilled Flank Steak

Servings:4 | Cooking Time: 10 Minutes

Ingredients:

- 1 (5-inch) piece fresh ginger, minced
- 3 tablespoons dark sesame oil
- 2 tablespoons Garlic Oil (here)
- 2 teaspoons lime juice
- 1 tablespoon brown sugar
- 2 teaspoons salt
- 1 teaspoon pepper
- 1½ pounds flank steak
- Oil for preparing the grill or grill pan

Directions:

1. In large bowl or resealable plastic bag, combine the ginger, sesame oil, Garlic Oil, lime juice, brown sugar, salt, and pepper. Add the steak and turn to coat. Marinate the meat at room temperature for 30 minutes.
2. To cook the steak, oil a grill or grill pan, and heat to medium-high heat. Remove the steak from the marinade and cook on the grill for 4 to 5 minutes per side for medium-rare (cook a minute or two longer per side for medium, and even longer for well-done).
3. Tent the cooked steak loosely with aluminum foil and let rest for 10 minutes before slicing.
4. To serve, slice the steak across the grain into ⅛-inch-thick slices and serve immediately.

Nutrition Info:

- Calories: 460; Protein: 48g; Total Fat: 25g; Saturated Fat: 8g; Carbohydrates: 9g; Fiber: 1g; Sodium: 1262mg;

Chicken And Rice With Peanut Sauce

Servings:4 | Cooking Time: 10 Minutes

Ingredients:
- 2 tablespoons Garlic Oil
- 1 pound boneless skinless chicken thigh meat, cut into strips
- ½ cup sugar-free natural peanut butter
- ½ cup coconut milk
- 2 tablespoons gluten-free soy sauce
- 1 tablespoon peeled and grated fresh ginger
- Juice of 1 lime
- 2 cups cooked brown rice

Directions:
1. In a large nonstick skillet over medium-high heat, heat the garlic oil until it shimmers.
2. Add the chicken and cook for about 6 minutes, stirring occasionally, until browned.
3. In a small bowl, whisk the peanut butter, coconut milk, soy sauce, ginger, and lime juice. Add this to the chicken.
4. Mix in the rice. Cook for 3 minutes more, stirring.

Nutrition Info:
- Calories:718; Total Fat: 40g; Saturated Fat: 13g; Carbohydrates: 46g; Fiber: 5g; Sodium: 757mg; Protein: 46g

Lamb And Vegetable Pilaf

Servings:4 | Cooking Time:x

Ingredients:
- 2 tablespoons olive oil
- 2 teaspoons garlic-infused olive oil
- 2½ teaspoons grated ginger
- 2 teaspoons ground cinnamon
- 6 whole cloves
- ½ teaspoon cayenne pepper
- 2 teaspoons ground cumin
- 1¼ pounds (500 g) boneless lamb loin, sliced
- 1½ cups (300 g) white basmati rice
- 1 small sweet potato, chopped
- 2½ cups (625 ml) gluten-free, onion-free beef or vegetable stock*
- ⅔ cup (65 g) slivered almonds
- 1 large eggplant, trimmed and sliced
- 2 medium zucchini, halved lengthwise and thickly sliced
- Salt and freshly ground black pepper
- ¼ cup (5 g) roughly chopped cilantro
- 3 tablespoons roughly chopped flat-leaf parsley

Directions:
1. Heat 1 tablespoon plus 2 teaspoons of the olive oil and the 2 teaspoons garlic-infused oil in a large saucepan or Dutch oven over medium heat. Add the ginger, cinnamon, cloves, cayenne, and cumin and cook for 1 to 2 minutes, until fragrant. Add the lamb and toss until browned.
2. Add the rice, sweet potato, and eggplant to the pan and cook, stirring, for 2 to 3 minutes, until the rice is well coated in the spiced oil. Pour in the stock and bring to a boil, then reduce the heat to low and simmer, covered, for 10 minutes.
3. Meanwhile, heat the remaining 1 teaspoon of olive oil in a small frying pan over medium heat. Add the almonds and cook, stirring, until golden. Drain on paper towels.
4. Add the zucchini to the rice mixture and cook for 5 minutes more, or until all the liquid has been absorbed and the rice is tender. Remove and discard the whole cloves. Season with salt and pepper, then stir in the almonds, cilantro, and parsley. Serve hot.

Nutrition Info:
- 630 calories; 24 g protein; 34 g total fat; 11 g saturated fat; 54 g carbohydrates; 7 g fiber; 318 mg sodium

Turkey And Red Pepper Burgers

Servings:4 | Cooking Time: 10 Minutes

Ingredients:

- 1 pound ground turkey
- ½ teaspoon sea salt
- ⅛ teaspoon freshly ground black pepper
- 2 tablespoons extra-virgin olive oil
- ¼ cup Low-FODMAP Mayonnaise
- 2 jarred roasted red peppers, minced
- 4 gluten-free hamburger buns

Directions:

1. Form the turkey into 4 patties and season them with salt and pepper.
2. In a large nonstick skillet over medium-high heat, heat the olive oil until it shimmers.
3. Add the burgers and cook for about 5 minutes per side, until browned.
4. In a small bowl, whisk the mayonnaise and red peppers. Spread the mixture on the buns and add the cooked patties.

Nutrition Info:

- Calories:468; Total Fat: 26g; Saturated Fat: 4g; Carbohydrates: 27g; Fiber: 1g; Sodium: 753mg; Protein: 36g

Turkey Quinoa Meatballs With Mozzarella

Servings:15 | Cooking Time:x

Ingredients:

- 1 cup cooked quinoa
- 1 pound ground lean turkey meat
- 2 large eggs
- ½ teaspoon freshly ground black pepper
- ½ teaspoon paprika
- ½ teaspoon dried oregano
- ½ teaspoon dried thyme
- ½ teaspoon dried parsley
- 8 ounces fresh mozzarella, cubed
- 2 tablespoons chopped fresh flat-leaf parsley
- ½ cup grated Parmesan cheese

Directions:

1. Preheat oven to 350°F. Line a baking sheet with parchment paper.
2. Mix all ingredients together (except mozzarella, parsley, and Parmesan cheese) in a large bowl.
3. Divide meat mixture into 15 portions.
4. Place 1 small mozzarella cube in the center of each portion and shape into a ball.
5. Bake 30 minutes or until meatballs are not pink inside.
6. Garnish with fresh parsley and Parmesan cheese.

Nutrition Info:

- Calories: 128,Fat: 8g,Protein: 11g,Sodium: 183mg,Carbohydrates: 3.

Garden Veggie Dip Burgers

Servings:4 | Cooking Time:x

Ingredients:

- 2 tablespoons light sour cream
- 1 large carrot, peeled and diced
- 1/2 medium red bell pepper, seeded and diced
- 1/2 cup packed baby spinach leaves, chopped
- 1 teaspoon sea salt
- 1 pound lean ground beef

Directions:

1. In a food processor, blend sour cream, carrot, pepper, spinach, and salt until creamy.
2. In a large bowl, add vegetable mixture to ground beef and mix to combine. Make 4 patties. Refrigerate patties for 12–24 hours before grilling.
3. Heat a charcoal or gas grill to 350°F. Cook patties on grill to an internal temperature of 160°F, about 5 minutes per side.

Nutrition Info:

- Calories: 177,Fat: 7g,Protein: 25g,Sodium: 680mg,Carbohydrates: 3.

Fish And Potato Pie

Servings:6 | Cooking Time: 50 Minutes

Ingredients:

- 2 large potatoes
- 4 tablespoons butter, divided
- 1½ teaspoons salt, divided
- 1 teaspoon freshly ground black pepper, divided
- ¾ pound smoked whitefish (such as haddock), cut into bite-size pieces
- ¾ pound skinless salmon fillet, cut into ½-inch pieces
- 1 medium carrot, coarsely grated
- 2 (8-inch) stalks celery, coarsely grated
- 4 cups chopped fresh spinach
- 4 ounces grated sharp white cheddar cheese

Directions:

1. Preheat the oven to 400°F.
2. Bring a pot of salted water to a boil. Add the potatoes and cook for 10 to 12 minutes, until the potatoes are tender. Drain and then mash the potatoes along with 2 tablespoons of the butter, ¾ teaspoon of the salt, and ½ teaspoon of the pepper.
3. In a large baking dish, toss together the smoked fish, salmon, carrot, celery, and spinach. Season with the remaining ¾ teaspoon salt and ½ teaspoon pepper. Spread the mixture out in an even layer. Spread the mashed potatoes over the top in an even layer. Melt the remaining 2 tablespoons of butter and drizzle it over the top. Sprinkle the cheese over the top.
4. Bake in the preheated oven for 30 to 40 minutes, until the top is golden brown and the dish is hot all the way through. Serve immediately.

Nutrition Info:

- Calories: 366; Protein: 34g; Total Fat: 16g; Saturated Fat: 10g; Carbohydrates: 22g; Fiber: 4g; Sodium: 1312mg;

Spanish Meatloaf With Garlic Mashed Potatoes

Servings:6 | Cooking Time:x

Ingredients:

- Nonstick cooking spray
- 1½ pounds (700 g) extra-lean ground beef
- ½ cup (125 ml) tomato paste
- ¾ cup (90 g) dried gluten-free, soy-free bread crumbs*
- 2 large eggs, lightly beaten
- 2 teaspoons garlic-infused olive oil
- 2 teaspoons olive oil
- Small handful of flat-leaf parsley leaves, roughly chopped
- ¾ teaspoon ground ginger
- 1 teaspoon chili powder
- 1½ teaspoons cayenne pepper
- 1½ teaspoons sweet paprika
- Salt and freshly ground black pepper
- 4 potatoes, peeled (if desired) and quartered
- 1 tablespoon garlic-infused olive oil
- 2 tablespoons (30 g) salted butter
- ⅓ cup (80 ml) low-fat milk, lactose-free milk, or suitable plant-based milk
- Salt and freshly ground black pepper
- Green salad or vegetables, for serving

Directions:

1. Preheat the oven to 350°F (180°C). Line an 8½ x 4½-inch (25 x 11.5 cm) loaf pan with foil and spray with cooking spray.
2. Combine the beef, tomato paste, bread crumbs, eggs, garlic-infused oil, olive oil, parsley, ginger, chili powder, cayenne, paprika, salt, and pepper in a large bowl. Mix well with your hands. Press into the loaf pan.
3. Bake for 40 to 45 minutes, until cooked through. (The juices will run clear when you pierce the center with a small knife.) Let rest for at least 5 minutes before serving.
4. Meanwhile, to make the garlic mashed potatoes, cook the potatoes in a saucepan of boiling water until very tender, about 10 minutes. Drain. Mash with a potato masher. Stir in the garlic-infused oil, butter, and milk and season with salt and pepper. Adjust the ingredients for taste or texture if needed.
5. Cut the meatloaf into thick slices and serve with a generous spoonful (or two) of mashed potatoes and your choice of salad or vegetables.

Nutrition Info:

- 437 calories; 29 g protein; 23 g total fat; 8 g saturated fat; 28 g carbohydrates; 3 g fiber; 370 mg sodium

Mexican-style Ground Beef And Rice

Servings:4 | Cooking Time: 15 Minutes

Ingredients:

- 2 tablespoons Garlic Oil
- 1 pound 85 percent lean ground beef (see Tip)
- 6 scallions, green parts only, chopped
- ½ cup water
- 1 tablespoon chili powder
- 1 teaspoon dried cumin
- ½ teaspoon sea salt
- ⅛ teaspoon freshly ground black pepper
- 2 cups cooked brown rice
- ¼ cup chopped fresh cilantro leaves

Directions:

1. In a large nonstick skillet over medium-high heat, heat the garlic oil until it shimmers.
2. Add the ground beef and scallions. Cook for about 6 minutes, crumbling the beef with the back of a spoon, until it is browned.
3. Stir in the water, chili powder, cumin, salt, and pepper. Cook for 2 minutes more, stirring, until the spices are mixed in.
4. Stir in the brown rice and cilantro. Cook for 2 minutes more to heat.

Nutrition Info:

- Calories:458; Total Fat: 16g; Saturated Fat: 4g; Carbohydrates: 39g; Fiber: 3g; Sodium: 335mg; Protein: 39g

Arroz Con Pollo With Olives, Raisins, And Pine Nuts

Servings:6 | Cooking Time: 60 Minutes

Ingredients:
- FOR THE CHICKEN
- 2 tablespoons orange juice
- 2 tablespoons lime juice
- 1½ teaspoons salt
- ¾ teaspoon freshly ground black pepper
- 1 whole chicken (about 3½ to 4½ pounds), cut into 8 serving pieces
- 1 tablespoon vegetable oil
- 1 tablespoon unsalted butter
- FOR THE RICE
- 2 green bell peppers, diced
- ¼ teaspoon saffron threads, soaked in ¼ cup warm water
- 2 teaspoons ground cumin
- 2 teaspoons salt
- 1 bay leaf
- 1 (14½-ounce) can diced onion- and garlic-free tomatoes with juice
- 1½ cups homemade (onion- and garlic-free) chicken broth
- 1¼ cups water
- 1½ cups long-grain white rice
- ½ cup golden raisins
- ½ cup small pimiento-stuffed green olives, rinsed
- ¼ cup toasted pine nuts (optional)

Directions:
1. To prepare the chicken, combine the orange juice, lime juice, salt, and pepper in a large bowl. Add the chicken and turn to coat. Cover and marinate in the refrigerator for at least 1 hour.
2. Remove the chicken from the marinade, reserving the marinade. Pat the chicken pieces dry with paper towels.
3. Heat the oil and butter in a large Dutch oven or stockpot over medium-high heat. Brown the chicken in batches for about 6 minutes per batch, until the chicken is browned on both sides. Transfer the browned chicken pieces to a large plate.
4. To make the rice, begin by preheating the oven to 350°F.
5. Add the bell peppers to the Dutch oven and sauté over medium-high heat, stirring occasionally, until the vegetables soften, for about 8 minutes. Add the saffron along with its soaking liquid, the cumin, salt, bay leaf, tomatoes along with their juice, broth, water, and the reserved marinade. Bring to a boil. Add the chicken pieces except for the breasts. Reduce the heat to low, cover, and simmer for 10 minutes. Stir in the rice and add the chicken breasts, skin-side up, on top of the rice and vegetables. Cover and transfer to the preheated oven. Cook for 20 minutes, until the rice is tender and the liquid has been absorbed.
6. Remove the pot from the oven and sprinkle the raisins, olives, and pine nuts (if using) over the top. Cover the pot with a clean dish towel and let rest for 5 to 10 minutes. Discard the bay leaf.

Nutrition Info:
- Calories: 651; Protein: 55g; Total Fat: 23g; Saturated Fat: 5g; Carbohydrates: 53g; Fiber: 3g; Sodium: 1725mg;

Lemon Thyme Chicken

Servings:3 | Cooking Time:x

Ingredients:
- 4 chicken thighs and 4 drumsticks (about 2 1/2 pounds)
- 3 medium lemons
- Zest of 1 medium lemon
- 1 tablespoon butter
- 1/4 teaspoon sea salt
- 1/2 teaspoon freshly ground black pepper
- 2 tablespoons fresh thyme leaves
- 6 basil leaves, torn

Directions:
1. Preheat oven to 375°F.
2. Add chicken to a large bowl. Slice lemons in half and juice into bowl.
3. Add lemon zest, butter, salt, pepper, and thyme; toss well with your hands. Place chicken in a 9" × 13" baking dish.
4. Bake 35–40 minutes, basting every 10 minutes. Skin should get crispy and meat should be cooked through.
5. Garnish with basil leaves.

Nutrition Info:
- Calories: 90,Fat: 5g,Protein: 6g,Sodium: 219mg,Carbohydrates: 9.

Turkey Bolognese With Pasta

Servings:4 | Cooking Time:x

Ingredients:

- 1 tablespoon olive oil
- 1 large carrot, peeled and diced small
- 1/8 teaspoon wheat-free asafetida powder
- 1 teaspoon salt, divided
- 1/2 teaspoon dried oregano
- 4 ounces pancetta, visible fat discarded and pancetta minced
- 1 pound ground turkey
- 2 tablespoons Tomato Paste (see Chapter 13)
- 1/2 cup Lambrusco wine
- 1 (14-ounce) can San Marzano tomatoes
- 1 tablespoon balsamic vinegar
- 1 pound gluten-free angel hair pasta
- 1/4 cup shaved Parmesan cheese

Directions:

1. Heat oil in a wide, deep skillet or saucepan over medium heat. Add carrots, asafetida, 1/2 teaspoon salt, and oregano and cook for 6 minutes. Add pancetta and continue cooking everything until carrots are softened, 8–10 minutes.
2. Add ground turkey and remaining 1/2 teaspoon salt. Cook until meat is lightly browned. Add tomato paste and cook 2–3 minutes.
3. Add wine. Cook until wine has reduced by half, 4–5 minutes.
4. Add tomatoes and stir. Cook 5 minutes. Stir balsamic vinegar into sauce. Set heat to low and simmer.
5. Meanwhile, cook pasta according to package directions. Drain. Stir Parmesan into pasta and top with Bolognese sauce.

Nutrition Info:

- Calories: 528,Fat: 18g,Protein: 40g,Sodium: 1,010mg,Carbohydrates: 93.

Roast Beef Tenderloin With Parmesan Crust

Servings:8 | Cooking Time:x

Ingredients:

- 1 (4-pound) center-cut beef tenderloin, fat and silver skin trimmed
- 1/4 teaspoon kosher salt
- 5 teaspoons freshly ground black pepper, divided
- 2/3 cup gluten-free fine bread crumbs
- 3/4 cup finely grated Parmesan cheese
- 2/3 cup Basic Mayonnaise (see Chapter 13)
- 1 tablespoon Dijon mustard
- 1 tablespoon finely grated lemon zest
- 1 tablespoon gluten-free Worcestershire sauce

Directions:

1. Season tenderloin lightly with salt and 1 teaspoon pepper. Wrap in plastic wrap and refrigerate overnight.
2. Uncover tenderloin; let stand at room temperature for up to 2 hours.
3. Preheat oven to 400°F.
4. Set a rack inside a rimmed baking sheet. Transfer tenderloin to rack.
5. In a small food processor, pulse 4 teaspoons black pepper and remaining ingredients until well blended. Using your hands, pack Parmesan mixture around tenderloin.
6. Roast until crust is golden brown, about 30–40 minutes for medium-rare. An instant-read thermometer inserted into the thickest part of the tenderloin should register 120°F–125°F.
7. Transfer to a carving board; cover loosely with foil and let rest 10 minutes. Cut into 1/2"-thick slices, being careful to keep the delicate crust in place.

Nutrition Info:

- Calories: 401,Fat: 24g,Protein: 37g,Sodium: 497mg,Carbohydrates: 6.

Smoky Sourdough Pizza

Servings:4 | Cooking Time:x

Ingredients:

- 2 tablespoons extra-virgin olive oil
- 2 garlic cloves, peeled, slightly smashed
- 8 pieces smoked sun-dried tomatoes, diced, divided
- 8 ounces smoked Brie, trimmed, cut to 1" cubes
- 6 ounces smoked ham, cut to 1/2" cubes
- 1 cup seeded, diced tomatoes
- 1/4 cup pitted, diced Kalamata olives
- 1/8 teaspoon sea salt
- 1/8 teaspoon freshly ground black pepper
- 1 gluten-free sourdough loaf, insides removed
- 1/2 cup freshly grated Parmesan cheese
- 1/2 cup thinly sliced kale leaves, stems removed

Directions:

1. Heat oven to 400°F. Line a baking sheet with parchment paper.
2. Heat oil in a small skillet over medium heat. Add garlic and half of the sun-dried tomatoes and stir until fragrant, about 1 minute. Remove from heat and set aside to cool. Once cool, remove and discard garlic.
3. Transfer oil with tomatoes to a medium bowl. Toss in remaining sun-dried tomatoes, Brie, ham, diced tomatoes, and olives. Season with salt and pepper and toss again.
4. Cut bread crust into 4 even pieces and place on baking sheet. Fill each piece with an even amount of the tomato/ham/ Brie mixture, spreading in an even layer. Top with Parmesan cheese and kale.
5. Bake 5–8 minutes or until crusts turn light brown and cheese melts.

Nutrition Info:

- Calories: 352,Fat: 26g,Protein: 22g,Sodium: 807mg,Carbohydrates: 7.5.

Spaghetti And Meat Sauce

Servings:4 | Cooking Time: 10 Minutes

Ingredients:

- 2 tablespoons Garlic Oil
- 1 pound ground beef
- 1 cup tomato sauce
- 1 teaspoon dried oregano
- 1 cup Low-FODMAP Poultry Broth
- 1 tablespoon cornstarch
- 1/2 teaspoon sea salt
- Pinch red pepper flakes
- 1/4 cup chopped fresh basil leaves
- 8 ounces gluten-free spaghetti, cooked according to the package directions and drained

Directions:

1. In a large nonstick skillet over medium-high heat, heat the garlic oil until it shimmers.
2. Add the ground beef and cook for about 6 minutes, crumbling it with the back of a spoon, until browned.
3. Stir in the tomato sauce and oregano.
4. In a small bowl, whisk together the broth, cornstarch, salt, and red pepper flakes. Add this to the skillet and cook for about 2 minutes, stirring, until the sauce begins to thicken.
5. Stir in the basil.
6. Toss with the hot spaghetti.

Nutrition Info:

- Calories:468; Total Fat: 16g; Saturated Fat: 4g; Carbohydrates: 37g; Fiber: 1g; Sodium: 835mg; Protein: 43g

Cumin Turkey With Fennel

Servings:4 | Cooking Time:x

Ingredients:
- 1 tablespoon brown sugar
- 1/4 teaspoon ground cinnamon
- 1/2 tablespoon ground cumin
- 1/4 teaspoon kosher salt
- 1/2 teaspoon freshly ground black pepper
- 1/4 teaspoon cayenne pepper
- 1 cup cubed celeriac
- 1 cup halved seedless red grapes
- 1 fennel bulb (about 1/2 pound), cut into 1" chunks
- 1 tablespoon olive oil
- 2 pounds lean turkey fillets

Directions:
1. Preheat oven to 425°F. Position rack in upper third of oven.
2. Mix brown sugar, cinnamon, cumin, salt, pepper, and cayenne in a small bowl.
3. In a medium bowl, combine celeriac, grapes, and fennel with oil and half of spice mixture. Spread out evenly in a single layer in an 18" × 13" rimmed baking sheet.
4. Rub remaining spice mixture on both sides of turkey fillets and place on top of grapes and vegetables.
5. Bake 40 minutes; check at 30 minutes to be sure food is not burning—if so, move pan to a lower rack.

Nutrition Info:
- Calories: 354,Fat: 7g,Protein: 52g,Sodium: 357mg,Carbohydrates: 19.

Mild Lamb Curry

Servings:6 | Cooking Time:x

Ingredients:
- ½ cup (75 g) cornstarch
- 2 pounds 10 ounces (1.2 kg) lean lamb steaks, cut into ¾-inch (2 cm) pieces
- 2 teaspoons garlic-infused olive oil
- 2 tablespoons rice bran oil or sunflower oil
- 2 teaspoons ground cinnamon
- 2 heaping tablespoons ground cumin
- 2 teaspoons ground ginger
- 1 heaping tablespoon ground turmeric
- 2 teaspoons paprika
- 1 teaspoon cayenne pepper
- 1 teaspoon salt
- 1 teaspoon freshly ground black pepper
- 4 cups (1 liter) gluten-free, onion-free beef stock*
- 2 heaping tablespoons light brown sugar
- One 14.5-ounce (425 g) can crushed tomatoes
- Steamed rice and cilantro leaves, for serving

Directions:
1. Place the cornstarch in a shallow bowl. Add the lamb pieces and toss to coat well. Shake off any excess.
2. Heat the garlic-infused oil and rice bran oil in a large heavy-bottomed saucepan or Dutch oven over medium heat. Add the cinnamon, cumin, ginger, turmeric, paprika, cayenne, salt, and pepper and cook for 1 to 2 minutes, until fragrant. Add the lamb and cook, stirring occasionally, for 5 to 7 minutes, until nicely browned. Add the stock and brown sugar and bring to a boil, then reduce the heat and simmer gently for 1½ hours, stirring occasionally.
3. Stir in the crushed tomatoes and cook for another hour or until the meat is very tender. Make sure the heat is kept very low so the lamb does not boil dry. (Add a little water if necessary.)
4. Season to taste with salt and pepper and serve with steamed rice, garnished with cilantro.

Nutrition Info:
- 538 calories; 27 g protein; 39 g total fat; 15 g saturated fat; 16 g carbohydrates; 2 g fiber; 647 mg sodium

Red Snapper With Sweet Potato Crust And Cilantro-lime Sauce

Servings:4 | Cooking Time: 15 Minutes

Ingredients:
- FOR THE SAUCE
- 1 cup chopped fresh cilantro
- Juice of 2 limes
- ½ cup olive oil
- 1 tablespoon Garlic Oil (here)
- 1 teaspoon salt
- ½ teaspoon freshly ground black pepper
- ½ teaspoon sugar
- FOR THE FISH
- ½ cup gluten-free all-purpose flour
- 1 egg plus 2 egg whites
- 4 (6-ounce) snapper fillets
- 1 teaspoon salt
- ½ teaspoon freshly ground black pepper
- 1 tablespoon grapeseed oil
- 2 tablespoons butter
- 2 sweet potatoes, peeled and shredded

Directions:

1. To make the sauce, combine the cilantro, lime juice, olive oil, Garlic Oil, salt, pepper, and sugar in a blender or food processor and process until smooth.

2. Preheat the oven to 375°F. Place the flour in a wide, shallow bowl. Beat together the egg and egg whites in a second wide, shallow bowl. Season the fish on both sides with salt and pepper.

3. To prepare the fish, heat the oil and butter in a large, oven-safe skillet over medium-high heat. Place a handful of sweet potatoes in the skillet, making a bed roughly the size and shape of each fish fillet. Dredge the fish fillets in the flour, then the egg, and set on top of the sweet potatoes. Cook until the sweet potatoes are crisp and golden brown, for about 4 minutes. Using a spatula, lift the crusted fish out of the pan, and use your other hand to create another bed of sweet potatoes. Flip the fish over onto the new sweet potato bed. Repeat with the other pieces of fish. Place the skillet in the preheated oven and cook for 5 to 7 minutes more, until the bottom crust is crisp and golden brown and the fish is cooked through.

4. Serve hot, with the sauce drizzled over the top.

Nutrition Info:
- Calories: 653; Protein: 49g; Total Fat: 39g; Saturated Fat: 8g; Carbohydrates: 26g; Fiber: 4g; Sodium: 1357mg;

Orange-ginger Salmon

Servings:4 | Cooking Time: 12 Minutes

Ingredients:
- ¼ cup Garlic Oil
- Juice of 2 oranges
- 2 tablespoons gluten-free soy sauce
- 1 tablespoon peeled and grated fresh ginger
- 1 pound salmon fillet, quartered

Directions:
1. Preheat the oven to 450°F.
2. In a shallow baking dish, whisk together the garlic oil, orange juice, soy sauce, and ginger.
3. Place the salmon, flesh-side down, in the marinade. Marinate for 10 minutes.
4. Place the salmon, skin-side up, on a rimmed baking sheet. Bake for 12 to 15 minutes, until opaque.

Nutrition Info:
- Calories:282; Total Fat: 20g; Saturated Fat: 3g; Carbohydrates: 5g; Fiber: 0g; Sodium: 553mg; Protein: 23g

Steamed Mussels With Saffron-infused Cream

Servings:4 | Cooking Time: 15 Minutes

Ingredients:

- 2 tablespoons olive oil
- 1 tablespoon Garlic Oil (here)
- 1 large bulb fennel, thinly sliced
- 1 cup dry white wine
- Large pinch saffron threads
- ¾ teaspoon salt
- ¾ cup heavy cream
- ¼ teaspoon freshly ground pepper
- 4 pounds cultivated mussels, rinsed well
- 2 tablespoons chopped fresh flat-leaf parsley

Directions:

1. Heat the olive oil and Garlic Oil in a stockpot over medium heat.
2. Add the fennel and cook, stirring frequently, until softened, for about 5 minutes. Add the wine, saffron, and salt, and bring to a boil. Stir in the cream, pepper, and mussels.
3. Cover the pot and cook for about 6 minutes or until all of the mussels have opened (discard any mussels that don't open after 8 minutes of cooking). Serve the mussels and broth in bowls, garnished with the parsley.

Nutrition Info:

- Calories: 599; Protein: 55g; Total Fat: 26g; Saturated Fat: 8g; Carbohydrates: 24g; Fiber: 2g; Sodium: 1779mg;

Turkey Pasta With Kale

Servings:2 | Cooking Time:x

Ingredients:

- 1/2 pound gluten-free pasta
- 2 cups chopped kale (thick ribs and stems removed)
- 1 tablespoon extra-virgin olive oil
- 1/16 teaspoon salt
- 1 tablespoon olive oil
- 1 large carrot, peeled and thinly sliced
- 1/2 medium stalk celery, thinly sliced
- 1 tablespoon dried oregano
- 1/2 teaspoon freshly ground black pepper
- 1 pound ground lean turkey meat
- 1/2 cup chicken stock
- 1 (13.5-ounce) can diced tomatoes
- 3 tablespoons chopped fresh flat-leaf parsley
- 6 black olives
- 3/4 cup grated mozzarella cheese

Directions:

1. Cook pasta according to package directions.
2. Meanwhile, add kale to a small bowl with extra-virgin olive oil and salt. Massage until leaves are soft. Set aside.
3. Heat a large saucepan with olive oil over medium-high heat. Add carrot, celery, oregano, and pepper; sauté until carrots are tender, about 8–10 minutes.
4. Add turkey and break up into bite-sized pieces with spatula. Cook until browned. Add stock, tomatoes, and parsley and reduce heat to low; cook covered 5 minutes.
5. Once pasta is cooked and drained, add to saucepan. Stir in kale, olives, and mozzarella and toss to combine. Remove from heat and cover 2 minutes, then serve.

Nutrition Info:

- Calories: 1,104,Fat: 46g,Protein: 68g,Sodium: 867mg,Carbohydrates: 103.

Zucchini Lasagna With Meat Sauce

Servings:5 | Cooking Time:x

Ingredients:

- 2 cups Roasted Tomato Sauce (see Chapter 13)
- 1 1/2 large zucchini, cut lengthwise into thin slices
- 1 tablespoon olive oil
- 10 ounces ground beef
- 1 small green bell pepper, seeded and diced
- 1 tablespoon dried oregano
- 1/2 cup plus 2 tablespoons tomato paste
- 2 tablespoons chopped fresh basil
- 1/4 cup red wine (like Cabernet Sauvignon)
- 4 cups baby spinach
- 2 cups grated mozzarella cheese
- 1/2 cup grated Parmesan cheese

Directions:

1. Preheat oven to 325°F.

2. Grease a 9" × 13" casserole dish. Pour in enough tomato sauce to lightly coat bottom of dish, a little less than 1/2 cup. Layer a few zucchini slices side by side in bottom of dish.

3. Heat oil in a large skillet over medium-high heat. Add beef, stir, and cook 5 minutes. Add green pepper and oregano. Once meat is no longer pink, stir in tomato paste, remaining tomato sauce, basil, and wine. Bring to a boil; reduce heat and simmer sauce 20 minutes, stirring frequently.

4. Spoon a layer of meat sauce over the zucchini in casserole dish. Add a layer of spinach and then mozzarella. Repeat same process one more time—layer zucchini, meat sauce, spinach, and mozzarella. Finish by topping with Parmesan cheese.

5. Cover dish with foil and bake 45 minutes. Remove foil; increase temperature to 350°F and bake an additional 12–15 minutes. Lasagna will be very hot; let stand 5 minutes before serving.

Nutrition Info:

- Calories: 387,Fat: 22g,Protein: 30g,Sodium: 1,270mg,Carbohydrates: 18.

Beef Rolls With Horseradish Cream

Servings:4 | Cooking Time:x

Ingredients:

- Nonstick cooking spray
- 1 1/2 pounds (675 g) flank, sirloin, or top round steak, trimmed of fat and cut into 4 pieces
- 2 ounces (60 g) baby spinach leaves (2 cups), rinsed, dried, and finely chopped
- 2 heaping tablespoons finely chopped pitted black olives
- 1/4 cup plus 1 tablespoon (75 g) reduced-fat cream cheese, at room temperature
- Salt and freshly ground black pepper
- 1 heaping tablespoon freshly grated horseradish
- Squeeze of fresh lemon juice
- 1/4 cup (60 ml) light cream
- 2 heaping tablespoons finely chopped flat-leaf parsley
- Salt and freshly ground black pepper
- Green salad or vegetables, for serving

Directions:

1. Preheat the oven to 350°F (180°C). Grease a baking dish with nonstick cooking spray.

2. Place each steak between two sheets of parchment or waxed paper and flatten with a meat tenderizer or rolling pin until the steak is about a third of its original thickness. Cut each steak in half to make 8 thin steaks. Set aside.

3. Mix together the spinach, olives, and cream cheese and season with salt and pepper. Place about 1 tablespoon of the cream cheese filling across the center of each steak portion and roll up to enclose the filling. Secure with a toothpick.

4. Place the rolls in the baking dish and bake for 10 minutes. Cover with foil and bake for 5 minutes more or until cooked through.

5. Meanwhile, to make the horseradish cream, combine all the ingredients in a small saucepan and simmer gently over medium-low heat for 5 to 8 minutes, until thickened slightly. (Don't let it boil.)

6. Serve 2 beef rolls per person with the horseradish cream and your choice of salad or vegetables.

Nutrition Info:

- 479 calories; 35 g protein; 36 g total fat; 16 g saturated fat; 3 g carbohydrates; 1 g fiber; 391 mg sodium

Pumpkin Maple Roast Chicken

Servings:4 | Cooking Time:x

Ingredients:

- 1 1/2 tablespoons butter
- 1 tablespoon canned pumpkin
- 1 tablespoon pure maple syrup
- 1 teaspoon ground cinnamon
- 1 teaspoon dried thyme
- 1/2 teaspoon sea salt
- 1/4 teaspoon freshly ground black pepper
- 1 (4-pound) whole chicken

Directions:

1. Preheat oven to 375°F.
2. Melt butter in a small saucepan. Stir in pumpkin, maple syrup, cinnamon, thyme, salt, and pepper. Refrigerate 10 minutes.
3. Cut small slit under skin on both sides of chicken breast and under legs. Once the pumpkin mixture is cool, generously rub it under skin and all over the top of skin. Place chicken, breast side up, on the rack of a roasting pan. Roast 50–60 minutes or until a meat thermometer registers 165°F at thickest part of thigh.
4. Tent with foil and let rest 5 minutes before carving.

Nutrition Info:

- Calories: 588,Fat: 18g,Protein: 96g,Sodium: 641mg,Carbohydrates: 4.

Chinese Chicken

Servings:4 | Cooking Time:x

Ingredients:

- 3/4 cup arrowroot powder
- 1/2 cup white wine, divided
- 1/2 cup gluten-free tamari, divided
- 1 pound boneless, skinless chicken breasts, cubed
- 1/2 teaspoon sugar
- 1/2 cup Basic Roast Chicken Stock (see recipe in Chapter 8)
- 2 tablespoons sesame oil, divided
- 1 teaspoon natural peanut butter
- 4 garlic cloves, peeled and slightly smashed
- 1 cup broccoli florets
- 1 cup sliced red bell pepper
- 2 cups cooked brown rice

Directions:

1. In a medium bowl, stir to combine arrowroot and 1/4 cup each of wine and tamari. Add chicken; stir to coat. Cover and refrigerate for 30 minutes.
2. Transfer chicken to a colander and drain marinade completely. Set chicken aside.
3. In a separate bowl, combine sugar, stock, and remaining wine and tamari.
4. In another small bowl, whisk 1 tablespoon oil and peanut butter.
5. Heat remaining oil over medium-high heat in a large wok or skillet. Add the garlic and sauté, stirring constantly, until softened and brown at the edges, about 2 minutes. Remove garlic from pan and discard, leaving oil.
6. Add chicken and stir-fry quickly, browning chicken on all sides—approximately 8–10 minutes. (Lower heat if chicken is browning too quickly.) Scrape up and discard any loose marinade bits. Once fully cooked through, transfer chicken to a plate and cover to keep warm.
7. Add broccoli and bell pepper to skillet and quickly stir-fry for 1 minute. Add stock and peanut butter mixtures and stir. Cover, then lower heat and simmer for 5–8 minutes, until vegetables are crisp-tender.
8. Divide rice, chicken, and vegetables in their sauce evenly among four plates and serve.

Nutrition Info:

- Calories: 458,Fat: 11g,Protein: 30g,Sodium: 2,014mg,Carbohydrates: 53.

Vegetarian And Vegan

The Balanced Low-FODMAP Diet
Cookbook for Beginners

Vegetarian And Vegan

Quinoa-stuffed Eggplant Roulades With Feta And Mint

Servings:4 | Cooking Time: 45 Minutes

Ingredients:

- 3 tablespoons olive oil, divided
- ½ cup uncooked quinoa, rinsed
- 1 cup water
- ¼ cup toasted pine nuts
- 2 medium eggplants, sliced lengthwise into ¼-inch-thick slices
- ½ teaspoon salt
- ½ teaspoon freshly ground black pepper
- 1½ cups onion- and garlic-free tomato sauce or marinara sauce (such as Rao's Sensitive Formula Marinara Sauce)
- 2 tablespoons chopped fresh mint
- ½ cup crumbled feta cheese

Directions:

1. Preheat the oven to 375°F.
2. Grease a large baking dish with 1 tablespoon of the olive oil.
3. In a small saucepan, combine the quinoa and water, and bring to a boil over high heat. Reduce the heat to low, cover, and simmer for about 15 minutes, until the water has evaporated and the quinoa is tender. Stir in the pine nuts.
4. While the quinoa is cooking, prepare the eggplant slices. Heat the remaining 2 tablespoons of olive oil in a large skillet over medium-high heat. Sprinkle the eggplant slices on both sides with salt and pepper, and add them to the pan, cooking in a single layer (you'll need to cook them in batches). Cook for about 3 minutes per side, until golden brown. Transfer the eggplant slices to a plate as they are cooked.
5. To make the roulades, lay an eggplant slice on your work surface and spoon some of the quinoa onto the bottom. Roll the eggplant up into a tube around the filling. Place the rolls as you complete them into a baking dish, and spoon the marinara sauce over the top. Sprinkle the mint and cheese over the roulades, and bake in the preheated oven until they are heated through and the sauce is bubbly, for about 15 minutes.

Nutrition Info:

- Calories: 422; Protein: 11g; Total Fat: 25g; Saturated Fat: 6g; Carbohydrates: 44g; Fiber: 14g; Sodium: 894mg;

Mediterranean Noodles

Servings:4 | Cooking Time:x

Ingredients:

- 1 medium eggplant
- 1/2 cup garlic-infused olive oil
- 1/2 teaspoon sea salt
- 2 teaspoons freshly ground black pepper
- 1 (12-ounce) package gluten-free fusilli, cooked, drained, and rinsed under cold water
- 20 grape tomatoes, halved
- 1/2 cup sliced black olives
- 20 fresh basil leaves, torn
- 1 teaspoon dried oregano
- Juice of 2 medium lemons
- 1/2 cup grated Parmesan cheese

Directions:

1. Preheat oven to 475°F.
2. Cut eggplant into chunks and place in a large bowl. Using your hands, toss eggplant with oil, salt, and black pepper.
3. Place eggplant in a single layer on a baking sheet. Bake 20 minutes, flipping halfway through baking. When done, remove from oven and allow to cool. Eggplant should be soft. Transfer back to large bowl along with cooked noodles.
4. Stir in tomatoes, olives, basil, oregano, lemon juice, and Parmesan and serve.

Nutrition Info:

- Calories: 470,Fat: 33g,Protein: 11g,Sodium: 680mg,Carbohydrates: 36.

Smoky Corn Chowder With Red Peppers

Servings:4 | Cooking Time: 45 Minutes

Ingredients:

- 1 tablespoon olive oil
- 1 tablespoon Garlic Oil (here)
- 1 (10-inch) stalk celery, diced
- 2 carrots, diced
- 1 leek (green part only), halved lengthwise and thinly sliced
- 2 red bell peppers, seeded and diced
- 4 Yukon Gold potatoes, diced (about 1 pound)
- 2 cups canned corn kernels, divided
- 4 cups homemade (onion- and garlic-free) vegetable broth
- 1 teaspoon ground cumin
- ½ teaspoon smoked paprika
- ⅛ teaspoon cayenne
- 1 teaspoon salt
- 1 cup rice milk
- 3 scallions, green parts only, thinly sliced

Directions:

1. Heat the olive oil and Garlic Oil in a stockpot over medium heat. Add the celery and carrots and cook, stirring occasionally, for about 5 minutes, until the vegetables begin to soften. Add the leek, red bell peppers, potatoes, 1 cup of the corn, broth, cumin, smoked paprika, cayenne, and salt, and bring to a boil. Reduce the heat to low and simmer for about 30 minutes, until the potatoes are very tender.

2. Using an immersion blender or in batches in a countertop blender, purée the soup.

3. Stir in the remaining cup of corn and the rice milk, and cook over low heat for about 10 minutes more, until the soup is heated through and the corn kernels are tender. Serve immediately, garnished with sliced scallions.

Nutrition Info:

- Calories: 355; Protein: 13g; Total Fat: 7g; Saturated Fat: 1g; Carbohydrates: 69g; Fiber: 8g; Sodium: 1416mg;

Mexican Risotto

Servings:6 | Cooking Time:x

Ingredients:

- 1⁄2 each large red, green, yellow, and orange bell peppers, seeded and chopped
- 1 cup frozen corn
- 1⁄4 teaspoon salt, divided
- 1⁄4 teaspoon freshly ground black pepper, divided
- 2 tablespoons butter
- 1 cup arborio rice
- 3 cups vegetable stock
- 1 cup white cooking wine
- 1⁄2 tablespoon ground cumin
- 2 teaspoons chili powder
- 1 teaspoon dried oregano
- 1 teaspoon ground coriander
- Juice of 1 large lime
- 1 cup shredded Cheddar cheese
- 1⁄3 cup chopped fresh cilantro
- 1 medium avocado, cut into sixths

Directions:

1. Coat a small saucepan with cooking spray and sauté peppers over medium-high heat. After about 5 minutes, add corn and season with 1⁄8 teaspoon salt and 1⁄8 teaspoon pepper. Cook peppers until slightly charred, about 8 minutes. Set aside.

2. Meanwhile, in a medium skillet over medium-high heat, melt butter and add rice; fry until translucent, stirring for about 2 minutes.

3. Slowly add 1⁄2 cup stock and continuously stir until rice has absorbed all liquid. Follow this process again in 1⁄2-cup increments until stock is gone and then move on to two 1⁄2-cup increments of wine. Rice should be creamy and tender after 25–35 minutes. If rice is not completely cooked through, add more stock or wine. When cooked through, stir in peppers.

4. In a small bowl, stir together cumin, chili powder, oregano, coriander, lime juice, 1⁄8 teaspoon salt, and 1⁄8 teaspoon pepper. Stir into cooked rice along with cheese.

5. Top each serving with some cilantro and 1 slice of avocado. Serve immediately.

Nutrition Info:

- Calories: 385,Fat: 12g,Protein: 12g,Sodium: 758mg,Carbohydrates: 48.

Baked Tofu And Vegetables

Servings:4 | Cooking Time:x

Ingredients:
- 2 (14-ounce) packages extra-firm tofu, pressed between paper towels and patted dry
- 2 tablespoons toasted sesame oil, divided
- 2 teaspoons sesame seeds
- 2 1/2 tablespoons gluten-free soy sauce (tamari), divided
- 7–8 cups chopped bok choy (about 8 stalks)
- 1 bunch scallions, diced, green part only
- 1 medium red bell pepper, seeded and diced
- 1/4 cup slivered almonds
- 2 tablespoons rice wine vinegar

Directions:
1. Preheat oven to 400°F. Grease a large rimmed baking sheet with cooking spray.
2. Cut tofu into 1" pieces and toss in a large bowl with 1 tablespoon sesame oil, sesame seeds, and 2 tablespoons soy sauce.
3. Spread in a single layer on the prepared baking sheet. Bake tofu on lower rack of oven. Bake until browned, 25–30 minutes, flipping once.
4. While tofu is baking, heat a large skillet on medium-high and coat with 1 tablespoon sesame oil.
5. Add bok choy, scallions, bell pepper, almonds, remaining 1/2 tablespoon soy sauce, and vinegar. Cook until bok choy is slightly tender, stirring frequently. Place in same bowl used to prepare tofu.
6. Once tofu is ready, add to vegetables in bowl and stir until combined. Divide into 4 bowls and serve.

Nutrition Info:
- Calories: 267,Fat: 16g,Protein: 18g,Sodium: 725mg,Carbohydrates: 12.

Coconut-curry Tofu With Vegetables

Servings:4 | Cooking Time: 25 Minutes

Ingredients:
- FOR THE SAUCE
- 1 cup canned coconut milk
- 2 tablespoons chopped fresh cilantro
- 1 tablespoon gluten-free, onion- and garlic-free curry powder
- 1 teaspoon brown sugar
- 1 teaspoon salt
- FOR THE TOFU AND VEGETABLES
- 1 tablespoon grapeseed oil
- 14 ounces extra-firm tofu, drained and cut into cubes
- 1 red bell pepper, sliced
- 1 zucchini, halved lengthwise and sliced
- 2 cups broccoli florets
- 1 bunch baby bok choy, cut into 2-inch pieces

Directions:
1. To make the sauce, in a small bowl, stir together the coconut milk, cilantro, curry powder, brown sugar, and salt.
2. To prepare the tofu and vegetables, heat the oil in a large skillet over high heat. Arrange the tofu in the pan in a single layer and cook, without stirring, for about 5 minutes, until it begins to brown on the bottom. Scrape the tofu from the pan with a spatula and continue to cook, stirring occasionally, until it is golden brown all over, for about 7 more minutes.
3. Add the bell pepper, zucchini, broccoli, and bok choy to the pan, along with the sauce mixture, and continue to cook, stirring, for about 8 to 10 minutes, until the vegetables are tender. Serve immediately.

Nutrition Info:
- Calories: 321; Protein: 16g; Total Fat: 25g; Saturated Fat: 14g; Carbohydrates: 17g; Fiber: 6g; Sodium: 756mg;

Vegan Potato Salad, Cypriot-style

Servings:6 | Cooking Time:x

Ingredients:

- 2½ pounds Cyprus or Yukon Gold potatoes, peeled
- Juice of 1 medium lemon
- 2 tablespoons extra-virgin olive oil
- ½ teaspoon sea salt
- 1 teaspoon freshly ground black pepper
- 1 tablespoon dried oregano
- 1 bunch fresh cilantro, roughly chopped
- ¼ cup chopped fresh flat-leaf parsley
- 3 scallions, chopped, green part only
- 1 tablespoon olive oil
- ¼ cup roughly chopped black olives
- 2 tablespoons capers, rinsed and drained

Directions:

1. In a shallow pan of salted boiling water, cook potatoes 25 minutes. Drain and set aside until cool, then slice into small chunks.
2. Place potatoes in a large bowl with lemon juice and extra-virgin olive oil. Add salt, pepper, and oregano. Toss to coat evenly.
3. Add cilantro, parsley, and scallions. Toss to mix.
4. Heat olive oil in a small skillet over medium heat. Add olives and capers and fry 3 minutes. Sprinkle over potatoes in bowl. Tastes best when served immediately, but can be stored in refrigerator in an airtight container up to 2 days.

Nutrition Info:

- Calories: 203,Fat: 8g,Protein: 4g,Sodium: 345mg,Carbohydrates: 32.

Mixed Grains, Seeds, And Vegetable Bowl

Servings:4 | Cooking Time:x

Ingredients:

- 2 medium sweet potatoes, peeled and cut into 2" chunks
- 2 tablespoons olive oil
- 1½ tablespoons balsamic vinegar
- ½ teaspoon dried rosemary
- ½ teaspoon dried thyme
- ½ teaspoon dried oregano
- 2 tablespoons pumpkin seeds
- 1⅓ of a whole fennel bulb, halved lengthwise and cut into quarters
- ½ cup brown rice, cooked
- ¾ cup red quinoa, rinsed and cooked
- 1 cup buckwheat, rinsed and cooked
- ½ tablespoon coconut oil
- 3 cups baby spinach

Directions:

1. Preheat oven to 375°F.
2. Place sweet potatoes in a medium bowl. Add oil, vinegar, rosemary, thyme, and oregano. Toss with hands to coat. Place on rimmed baking sheet and roast 1 hour, flipping halfway through cooking and adding pumpkin seeds and fennel.
3. Add rice, quinoa, and buckwheat to same bowl used to prepare sweet potatoes. Stir in coconut oil.
4. Once sweet potatoes have finished baking and are tender, immediately add to bowl. Add spinach and toss. Serve immediately.

Nutrition Info:

- Calories: 411,Fat: 14g,Protein: 12g,Sodium: 72mg,Carbohydrates: 63.

Pasta With Pesto Sauce

Servings:4 | Cooking Time: 0 Minutes

Ingredients:
- 8 ounces gluten-free angel hair pasta, cooked according to the package instructions. Drained
- 1 recipe Macadamia Spinach Pesto
- ¼ cup grated Parmesan cheese

Directions:
1. In the warm pot that you used to cook the pasta, toss the noodles with the pesto.
2. Sprinkle with the cheese.

Nutrition Info:
- Calories:449; Total Fat: 25g; Saturated Fat: 6g; Carbohydrates: 46g; Fiber: 3g; Sodium: 444mg; Protein: 13g

Roasted-veggie Gyros With Tzatziki Sauce

Servings:4 | Cooking Time: 35 Minutes

Ingredients:
- FOR THE ROASTED VEGETABLES
- 1 large zucchini, chopped into half moons
- 1 large yellow squash, chopped into half moons
- 1 large eggplant, cut into 1-inch cubes
- 1 cup cherry tomatoes, halved
- ¼ cup olive oil
- 1 tablespoon chopped fresh oregano
- 1½ teaspoons salt
- ¾ teaspoon freshly ground black pepper
- FOR THE SAUCE
- 1 medium cucumber, peeled, seeded, coarsely grated and squeezed in a clean dish towel to remove excess moisture
- 8 ounces plain lactose-free yogurt
- 1 tablespoon Garlic Oil (here)
- 1 tablespoon white-wine vinegar
- 1 tablespoon chopped fresh dill
- 1 tablespoon lemon juice
- TO SERVE
- 4 gluten-free pita pockets or gluten-free naan
- 4 large lettuce leaves

Directions:
1. Preheat the oven to 425°F.
2. On a large, rimmed baking sheet, toss the zucchini, yellow squash, eggplant, and cherry tomatoes together with the olive oil, oregano, salt, and pepper. Spread the vegetables out in an even layer and roast in the preheated oven for about 35 minutes, until they are soft and browned.
3. While the vegetables are roasting, make the sauce. In a medium bowl, combine the cucumber, yogurt, Garlic Oil, vinegar, dill, and lemon juice, and stir to combine. Refrigerate, covered, until ready to serve.
4. Wrap the pitas in foil and heat in the oven (you can place them in the oven along with the vegetables while they're roasting) for about 10 minutes.
5. To serve, fill each pita with the roasted vegetables, top with a dollop of the tzatziki sauce, and garnish each with a lettuce leaf. Serve immediately.

Nutrition Info:
- Calories: 342; Protein: 14g; Total Fat: 15g; Saturated Fat: 2g; Carbohydrates: 46g; Fiber: 12g; Sodium: 1023mg;

Crustless Spinach Quiche

Servings:4 | Cooking Time: 20 Minutes

Ingredients:

- Nonstick cooking spray
- 6 eggs, beaten
- ¼ cup unsweetened almond milk
- ½ teaspoon sea salt
- ⅛ teaspoon freshly ground black pepper
- 1 teaspoon dried thyme
- 2 cups (2 [8-ounce] boxes) frozen spinach, thawed and squeezed of excess moisture
- ½ cup grated Swiss cheese

Directions:

1. Preheat the oven to 350°F.
2. Spray a 9-inch pie pan with nonstick cooking spray.
3. In a medium bowl, whisk together the eggs, almond milk, salt, pepper, and thyme.
4. Fold in the spinach and cheese. Pour the mixture into the prepared pie pan.
5. Bake for 20 to 25 minutes, until the quiche sets.

Nutrition Info:

- Calories:187; Total Fat: 14g; Saturated Fat: 8g; Carbohydrates: 3g; Fiber: <1g; Sodium: 368mg; Protein: 13g

Stuffed Zucchini Boats

Servings:4 | Cooking Time: 40 Minutes

Ingredients:

- 4 medium zucchini, halved lengthwise with the middles scooped out, chopped, and reserved
- 2 cups cooked brown rice
- ½ cup canned crushed tomatoes, drained
- ½ cup grated Parmesan cheese
- ¼ cup chopped fresh basil leaves
- ½ teaspoon sea salt
- ⅛ teaspoon freshly ground black pepper

Directions:

1. Preheat the oven to 400°F.
2. Place the zucchini halves on a rimmed baking sheet, cut-side up.
3. In a medium bowl, stir together the brown rice, reserved chopped zucchini, tomatoes, Parmesan cheese, basil, salt, and pepper. Spoon the mixture into the zucchini boats.
4. Bake for 40 to 45 minutes, until the zucchini are soft.

Nutrition Info:

- Calories:262; Total Fat: 5g; Saturated Fat: 2g; Carbohydrates: 46g; Fiber: 5g; Sodium: 447mg; Protein: 11g

Vegan Pad Thai

Servings:2 | Cooking Time:x

Ingredients:
- 2 1/2 cups water, divided
- 1 (10-ounce) package rice noodles or ramen-style noodles
- 2 tablespoons peanut butter
- Juice of 2 medium limes
- 3 tablespoons palm sugar
- 1 chili (about 4" long), chopped and seeded
- 4 tablespoons gluten-free soy sauce (tamari), divided
- 2 tablespoons garlic-infused olive oil
- 1/2 (12-ounce package) extra-firm tofu, drained and cut into cubes
- 1 medium head broccoli, florets chopped small
- 2 cups bean sprouts
- 1 large scallion, green part only
- 2 tablespoons chopped unsalted peanuts

Directions:
1. Bring 1 1/2 cups water to boil in a medium pot and submerge noodles to soak. Turn off heat.
2. In a small bowl, whisk together peanut butter, lime juice, sugar, chili, 3 tablespoons soy sauce, and 1 cup water.
3. In a large frying pan, heat oil on medium and add tofu. Drizzle 1 tablespoon soy sauce over tofu and sauté until golden brown. Add broccoli and bean sprouts. Cook 4–5 minutes.
4. Drain noodles. Add peanut butter mixture and stir well. Add to tofu and cook through, about 5 minutes.
5. Garnish with scallions and peanuts. Serve immediately.

Nutrition Info:
- Calories: 454,Fat: 13g,Protein: 16g,Sodium: 920mg,Carbohydrates: 73.

Collard Green Wraps With Thai Peanut Dressing

Servings:3 | Cooking Time:x

Ingredients:
- 1/4 teaspoon salt
- 2 teaspoons lemon juice
- 6 large collard green leaves
- 9 ounces semi-firm tofu
- 2/3 cup bean sprouts
- 2 medium carrots, peeled and julienned
- 1 medium cucumber, peeled and julienned
- 2 tablespoons chopped fresh cilantro leaves
- 1/2 small avocado
- Thai Peanut Dressing (see Chapter 13)

Directions:
1. Set a wide saucepan over high heat. Fill with 3" of water. Add salt and lemon juice. Bring water to a simmer and reduce heat to medium. Place 1 collard green leaf at a time in water 35–45 seconds. When leaves are done, they should turn a bright-colored green. When done with each leaf, remove from water and place on a plate with paper towels to cool.
2. Place 1 1/2 ounces tofu toward top of each collard green leaf. Top each with an equal amount sprouts, carrots, cucumber, and cilantro. Cut out three (1/8) portions of avocado and place over vegetables. Drizzle Thai peanut dressing over vegetables.
3. Roll up wraps like you would a burrito, tucking in sides as you roll. Slice rolls in half and serve.

Nutrition Info:
- Calories: 255,Fat: 13g,Protein: 14g,Sodium: 713mg,Carbohydrates: 27.

Peanut Butter Soba Noodles

Servings:4 | Cooking Time: 0 Minutes

Ingredients:

- 6 tablespoons sugar-free natural peanut butter
- ¼ cup low-sodium gluten-free soy sauce
- 2 tablespoons freshly squeezed lime juice
- 1 tablespoon Garlic Oil

- 1 teaspoon peeled and grated fresh ginger
- 1 packet stevia
- 8 ounces soba noodles, cooked according to the package directions, drained, and hot

Directions:

1. In a small bowl (or a blender), whisk together the peanut butter, soy sauce, lime juice, garlic oil, ginger, and stevia until smooth.
2. In a large serving bowl, combine the hot noodles and sauce and toss to coat.

Nutrition Info:

- Calories:357; Total Fat: 13g; Saturated Fat: 3g; Carbohydrates: 49g; Fiber: 2g; Sodium: 1,501mg; Protein: 17g

Latin Quinoa-stuffed Peppers

Servings:4 | Cooking Time:x

Ingredients:

- ½ cup quinoa
- 1 cup Vegetable Stock (see Chapter 4)
- 3 tablespoons nutritional yeast
- 2 cups spinach
- 2 teaspoons ground cumin
- 1 tablespoon chili powder
- 1 cup whole-kernel corn, drained

- 2 tablespoons macadamia nuts
- 4 large red, yellow, green, or orange bell peppers, tops cut off, seeds removed, halved
- 2 tablespoons coconut oil
- ½ ripe medium avocado, sliced into eighths
- 1 tablespoon fresh lime juice

Directions:

1. Preheat oven to 375°F and lightly grease a 9" × 13" baking dish or rimmed baking sheet with cooking spray.
2. Combine quinoa with stock in a medium saucepan. Bring to a boil. Cover, reduce heat to low, and simmer 15 minutes or until quinoa is tender.
3. Add cooked quinoa to a large mixing bowl and thoroughly mix together with yeast, spinach, cumin, chili powder, corn, and macadamia nuts.
4. Place peppers in baking dish and brush with coconut oil. Stuff peppers with quinoa mixture. Make sure none of the spinach is showing. Cover dish with foil.
5. Bake 30 minutes, then remove foil and increase heat to 400°F; bake another 30 minutes.
6. Top with avocado, then lime juice. Serve immediately.

Nutrition Info:

- Calories: 418,Fat: 22g,Protein: 14g,Sodium: 1,188mg,Carbohydrates: 46.

Chipotle Tofu And Sweet Potato Tacos With Avocado Salsa

Servings:4 | Cooking Time: 20 Minutes

Ingredients:
- FOR THE FILLING
- 2 tablespoons olive oil
- 2 sweet potatoes, peeled and cut into ½-inch cubes
- 1 pound firm tofu, diced
- ½ to 1 teaspoon ground chipotle chiles
- 2 tablespoons sugar
- Juice of 1 lime
- FOR THE AVOCADO SALSA
- 2 tomatoes
- ½ avocado, diced
- ¼ serrano chile, diced
- Juice of ½ lime
- ¼ teaspoon salt
- 2 tablespoons chopped fresh cilantro
- TO SERVE
- 8 soft corn tortillas

Directions:

1. Heat the olive oil in a large skillet over medium heat. Add the sweet potatoes and cook for about 5 minutes, until the potatoes begin to soften. Add the tofu, chipotle, sugar, and lime juice. Reduce the heat to low and cook, stirring occasionally, until the sweet potatoes are tender, about 15 minutes.
2. Meanwhile, wrap the tortillas in aluminum foil and heat them in a 350°F oven for 10 minutes.
3. To make the avocado salsa, combine the tomatoes, avocado, chile, lime juice, and salt in a medium bowl. Stir in the cilantro.
4. To serve, fill the tortillas with the filliing, dividing equally, and spoon a dollop of avocado salsa on top of each. Serve immediately.

Nutrition Info:
- Calories: 421; Protein: 15g; Total Fat: 18g; Saturated Fat: 3g; Carbohydrates: 55g; Fiber: 10g; Sodium: 229mg;

Lentil-walnut Burgers

Servings:6 | Cooking Time: 10 Minutes

Ingredients:
- 1½ cups canned lentils, rinsed and drained
- 1 tablespoon homemade (onion- and garlic-free) vegetable broth or water
- 2 teaspoons olive oil
- 8 ounces fresh baby spinach
- Juice of ½ lemon
- 1 teaspoon salt, divided
- ½ teaspoon freshly ground black pepper
- ½ teaspoon ground cumin
- 1 cup gluten-free bread crumbs
- ½ cup walnuts, toasted and finely chopped
- Cooking spray
- TO SERVE
- 6 gluten-free hamburger buns
- 2 cups baby arugula
- 1 large tomato, sliced
- 2 tablespoons spicy mustard

Directions:

1. In a medium bowl, mash the lentils with a potato masher, adding the tablespoon of broth or water.
2. Heat the oil in a large skillet set over medium heat. Add the spinach, lemon juice, ¼ teaspoon of the salt, pepper, and cumin and cook, stirring, until the spinach is cooked, about 3 minutes.
3. Add the spinach mixture, bread crumbs, walnuts, and the remaining ¾ teaspoon of salt to the mashed lentils, and stir to mix well. Refrigerate, covered, for at least 1 hour.
4. Coat a grill or grill pan with cooking spray and heat it to medium-high heat. Shape the lentil mixture into six patties, each about 4 inches across. Cook the patties for about 3 minutes on each side, until grill marks appear. Serve the patties hot on gluten-free buns, garnished with arugula, tomato, and spicy mustard.

Nutrition Info:
- Calories: 292; Protein: 13g; Total Fat: 6g; Saturated Fat: 1g; Carbohydrates: 48g; Fiber: 7g; Sodium: 764mg;

Cheese Strata

Servings:4 | Cooking Time: 30 Minutes

Ingredients:
- Nonstick cooking spray
- 3 eggs, beaten
- 1 cup unsweetened almond milk
- ½ teaspoon sea salt
- ⅛ teaspoon freshly ground black pepper
- 5 slices gluten-free sandwich bread, crusts removed, cut into cubes
- ¾ cup grated Monterey Jack cheese

Directions:
1. Preheat the oven to 350°F.
2. Spray a 9-by-5-inch loaf pan with nonstick cooking spray.
3. In a medium bowl, whisk together the eggs, almond milk, salt, and pepper.
4. Fold in the bread until it is coated with the egg mixture.
5. Fold in the cheese.
6. Pour the mixture into the prepared dish and bake for 30 to 35 minutes, until set.

Nutrition Info:
- Calories:402; Total Fat: 29g; Saturated Fat: 18g; Carbohydrates: 28g; Fiber: 6g; Sodium: 628mg; Protein: 12g

Mac 'n' Cheeze

Servings:4 | Cooking Time:x

Ingredients:
- 1 pound brown rice pasta noodles
- 3 tablespoons nutritional yeast
- 1/2 teaspoon sea salt, divided
- 1/4 cup coconut oil
- 1/4 cup sweet rice flour
- 23/4 cups unsweetened almond milk
- 1 teaspoon rice wine vinegar
- 1/2 cup dairy-free cheese shreds
- 1/4 teaspoon freshly ground black pepper
- 1 teaspoon paprika

Directions:
1. Bring a large pot of salted water to a rolling boil and cook pasta until al dente according to package directions. Drain and set aside.
2. In a small bowl, combine yeast and 1/4 teaspoon sea salt. Set aside.
3. In a large skillet, heat coconut oil over medium-low heat. Whisk in flour and continue whisking constantly 3–5 minutes or until flour smells toasty but hasn't browned.
4. In a steady stream, whisk in almond milk, stirring constantly. Add yeast mixture and vinegar. Cook 3 minutes or until slightly thickened.
5. Add cheese shreds and mix until well incorporated.
6. Add pasta and toss with sauce, black pepper, and remaining salt. Cook 1–2 minutes more to reheat pasta. Sprinkle on paprika. Serve immediately.

Nutrition Info:
- Calories: 574,Fat: 16g,Protein: 13g,Sodium: 646mg,Carbohydrates: 91.

Vegan Noodles With Gingered Coconut Sauce

Servings:4 | Cooking Time: 10 Minutes

Ingredients:
- 1 tablespoon Garlic Oil (here)
- 2½ tablespoons minced fresh ginger
- 1 (15-ounce) can light coconut milk
- 2 teaspoons sugar
- 2 teaspoons lemon juice
- 1 teaspoon salt
- ½ teaspoon freshly ground black pepper
- Red pepper flakes, to taste
- 1 bunch of Swiss chard leaves, thick center stems removed, leaves julienned
- 2 cups baby spinach
- 1 (16-ounce) package gluten-free spaghetti, cooked al dente according to package directions and drained
- 2 tablespoons chopped fresh basil

Directions:
1. Heat the Garlic Oil in a large sauté pan over medium heat. Add the ginger and cook, stirring, for about 3 minutes. Stir in the coconut milk, sugar, lemon juice, salt, pepper, and red pepper flakes and bring just to a boil. Reduce the heat to medium low and add the chard and spinach to the simmering sauce. Cook, stirring occasionally, until the greens are completely wilted, about 5 minutes.
2. Transfer the sauce mixture to a blender and purée, or transfer it to a bowl and purée it using an immersion blender.
3. Return the puréed sauce to the pan and bring it back to a simmer over medium heat. Add the prepared noodles and cook, stirring, until heated through, about 2 to 3 minutes. Serve immediately, garnished with basil.

Nutrition Info:
- Calories: 569; Protein: 11g; Total Fat: 15g; Saturated Fat: 1g; Carbohydrates: 99g; Fiber: 8g; Sodium: 908mg;

Vegetable Stir-fry

Servings:4 | Cooking Time: 10 Minutes

Ingredients:
- 2 tablespoons Garlic Oil
- 2⅔ cups chopped firm tofu
- 8 scallions, green parts only, chopped
- 2 cups broccoli florets
- ½ cup Stir-Fry Sauce

Directions:
1. In a large skillet over medium-high heat, heat the garlic oil until it shimmers.
2. Add the tofu, scallions, and broccoli. Cook for about 7 minutes, stirring frequently, until the broccoli is crisp-tender.
3. Stir in the stir-fry sauce. Cook for about 3 minutes, stirring, until it thickens.

Nutrition Info:
- Calories:231; Total Fat: 14g; Saturated Fat: 3g; Carbohydrates: 14g; Fiber: 4g; Sodium: 426mg; Protein: 16g

Vegetable And Rice Noodle Bowl

Servings:2 | Cooking Time:x

Ingredients:

- For the teriyaki sauce:
- 1⁄4 cup rice wine vinegar
- 1 tablespoon sesame oil
- 1 tablespoon light brown sugar
- 1⁄16 teaspoon wheat-free asafetida powder
- 11⁄2 teaspoons minced fresh gingerroot
- 1⁄4 teaspoon red pepper flakes
- 1 teaspoon freshly ground black pepper

- For the noodles:
- 1 tablespoon coconut oil
- 2 cups finely chopped broccoli florets
- 1 small stalk celery, chopped
- 2 medium carrots, peeled and shredded
- 3 ounces rice noodles, cooked and drained
- 1 scallion, chopped, green part only
- 2 teaspoons toasted sesame seeds

Directions:

1. In a medium bowl, whisk together all sauce ingredients until combined. Set aside.
2. Preheat a wok over medium-high heat. Add oil to coat pan. Add broccoli, celery, carrots, and 2 tablespoons of teriyaki sauce. Sauté about 8 minutes.
3. Stir drained noodles into wok along with remaining teriyaki sauce. Cook 2–3 minutes and serve immediately garnished with scallions and sesame seeds.

Nutrition Info:

- Calories: 281,Fat: 16g,Protein: 4g,Sodium: 92mg,Carbohydrates: 32.

Watercress Zucchini Soup

Servings:4 | Cooking Time: 15 Minutes

Ingredients:

- 2 tablespoons extra-virgin olive oil
- 1 leek, white part removed and the greens finely chopped
- 3 cups homemade (onion- and garlic-free) vegetable broth
- 1 pound zucchini, chopped
- 8 ounces chopped watercress

- 2 tablespoons dried tarragon
- 1 teaspoon salt
- 1⁄4 teaspoon freshly ground black pepper
- 2 tablespoons heavy cream

Directions:

1. In a large pot, heat the olive oil over medium-high heat until it shimmers.
2. Add the leek greens and cook, stirring occasionally, until the vegetables are soft, about seven minutes.
3. Add the vegetable broth and zucchini and simmer, stirring occasionally, for eight minutes.
4. Add the watercress, tarragon, salt, and pepper. Cook, stirring occasionally, an additional five minutes.
5. Carefully transfer the soup mixture to a blender or food processor. You may need to work in batches.
6. Fold a towel and place it over the top of the blender with your hand on top of it. Purée the soup for 30 seconds, and then remove the lid to vent steam. Close the blender and purée for another 30 seconds, until the mixture is smooth.
7. Transfer the mixture back to the cooking pot and stir in the heavy cream. Serve immediately.

Nutrition Info:

- Calories: 161; Total Fat: 11g; Saturated Fat: 3g; Cholesterol: 10mg; Carbohydrates: 9g; Fiber: 2g; Protein: 7g;

Spanish Rice

Servings:4 | Cooking Time: 10 Minutes

Ingredients:
- 2 tablespoons Garlic Oil
- 6 scallions, green parts only, chopped
- 2 cups hot cooked brown rice
- 1 cup canned crushed tomatoes, drained
- ½ cup Low-FODMAP Vegetable Broth
- ½ cup chopped black olives
- ½ cup pine nuts
- 1 teaspoon dried oregano
- ½ teaspoon sea salt
- ¼ teaspoon freshly ground black pepper

Directions:
1. In a large skillet over medium-high heat, heat the garlic oil until it shimmers.
2. Add the scallions. Cook for 3 minutes, stirring occasionally.
3. Stir in the brown rice, tomatoes, broth, olives, pine nuts, oregano, salt, and pepper. Cook for about 5 minutes more, stirring, until warmed through.

Nutrition Info:
- Calories:399; Total Fat: 22g; Saturated Fat: 2g; Carbohydrates: 46g; Fiber: 6g; Sodium: 506mg; Protein: 8g

Pineapple Fried Rice

Servings:4 | Cooking Time: 10 Minutes

Ingredients:
- 2 tablespoons Garlic Oil
- 6 scallions, green parts only, finely chopped
- ½ cup canned water chestnuts, drained
- 1 tablespoon peeled and grated fresh ginger
- 3 cups cooked brown rice
- 2 cups canned pineapple (in juice), drained, ¼ cup juice reserved
- 2 tablespoons gluten-free soy sauce
- ¼ cup chopped fresh cilantro leaves

Directions:
1. In a large skillet over medium-high heat, heat the garlic oil until it shimmers.
2. Add the scallions, water chestnuts, and ginger. Cook for 5 minutes, stirring.
3. Add the brown rice, pineapple, reserved pineapple juice, and soy sauce. Cook for 5 minutes, stirring, until the rice is warmed through.
4. Stir in the cilantro.

Nutrition Info:
- Calories:413; Total Fat: 9g; Saturated Fat: 1g; Carbohydrates: 77g; Fiber: 4g; Sodium: 396mg; Protein: 7g

Soups, Salads And Sides

Soups, Salads And Sides

Turkey-ginger Soup

Servings:4 | Cooking Time:17 Minutes

Ingredients:

- 2 tablespoons Garlic Oil
- 1 pound ground turkey
- 6 scallions, green parts only, chopped
- 2 carrots, chopped
- 2 tablespoons peeled, minced fresh ginger
- 7 cups Low-FODMAP Poultry Broth
- ½ teaspoon sea salt
- ⅛ teaspoon freshly ground black pepper
- 2 cups cooked brown rice

Directions:

1. In a large pot over medium-high heat, heat the garlic oil until it shimmers.
2. Add the turkey. Cook for about 5 minutes, crumbling it with the back of a spoon, until browned.
3. Add the scallions, carrots, and ginger. Cook for 3 minutes, stirring.
4. Stir in the broth, salt, and pepper. Bring to a simmer. Cook for about 7 minutes, until the carrots soften.
5. Stir in the brown rice and cook for 2 minutes more to heat through.

Nutrition Info:

- Calories: 482,Total Fat: 16g,Carbohydrates: 44g,Sodium: 610mg,Protein: 44.

Mussels In Chili, Bacon, And Tomato Broth

Servings:4 | Cooking Time:x

Ingredients:

- 4 ounces (113 g) lean bacon slices, cut crosswise into thin strips
- 2 tablespoons olive oil
- 3 cups (750 ml) tomato puree
- ½ teaspoon cayenne pepper (or to taste)
- 6½ cups (1.5 liters) reduced sodium gluten-free, onion-free chicken stock*
- 5½ pounds (2.5 kg) mussels, scrubbed and debearded
- Salt and freshly ground black pepper
- Gluten-free bread, for serving

Directions:

1. In a large heavy-bottomed saucepan over medium heat, cook the bacon until just golden. Spoon out and discard any excess fat, then add the olive oil, tomato puree, cayenne, and 2 cups (500 ml) of the stock. Bring to a boil, reduce the heat to low, and simmer for 30 to 40 minutes to develop the smoky bacon flavor.
2. Add the remaining stock. Increase the heat to medium-high and bring to a boil. Add the mussels and cook, covered, for 5 to 8 minutes, until all the mussels have opened. Shake the pan to redistribute the mussels and cook for an extra minute. Shake again. Discard any unopened mussels. Season to taste with salt and pepper and serve immediately with plenty of gluten-free bread to mop up the delicious broth.

Nutrition Info:

- : 612 calories,59 g protein,26 g total fat,33 g carbohydrates,2082 mg sodiu.

Chicken Noodle Soup

Servings:4 | Cooking Time:15 Minutes

Ingredients:

- 2 tablespoons Garlic Oil
- 6 scallions, green parts only, chopped
- 3 carrots, chopped
- 1 red bell pepper, chopped
- 6 cups Low-FODMAP Poultry Broth
- ½ teaspoon sea salt
- ⅛ teaspoon freshly ground black pepper
- 4 ounces gluten-free spaghetti, cooked according to instructions on package
- 4 cups chopped cooked chicken

Directions:

1. In a large pot over medium-high heat, heat the garlic oil until it shimmers.
2. Add the scallions, carrots, and bell pepper. Cook for 3 minutes, stirring occasionally.
3. Stir in the broth, salt, and pepper. Bring to a boil.
4. Add the spaghetti. Cook for 8 to 10 minutes, stirring occasionally, until the pasta is cooked. Drain.
5. Stir in the chicken. Cook for 2 minutes more.

Nutrition Info:

- Calories: 441,Total Fat: 35g,Carbohydrates: 24g,Sodium: 560mg,Protein: 52.

Greek Pasta Salad

Servings:6 | Cooking Time:x

Ingredients:

- 1 (12-ounce) package gluten-free rice spiral pasta
- ¼ cup garlic-infused olive oil
- ¼ cup extra-virgin olive oil
- 1 large lemon, juiced
- ⅓ cup rice wine vinegar
- 2 teaspoons dried oregano
- ⅛ teaspoon sea salt
- ¼ teaspoon freshly ground black pepper
- 1 (10-ounce) bag fresh spinach, rinsed, drained, and coarsely chopped
- 8 ounces feta cheese, crumbled
- 1 pint grape tomatoes, halved
- ½ cup pitted Kalamata olives

Directions:

1. Cook pasta according to package directions; drain and rinse.
2. Make dressing: In a large bowl, whisk together oils, lemon juice, vinegar, oregano, salt, and pepper.
3. Add spinach, feta, tomatoes, and olives to the bowl.
4. Add pasta and toss gently until evenly coated. Can be made ahead and covered in refrigerator up to 1 day.

Nutrition Info:

- Calories: 495,Fat: 26g,Protein: 9g,Sodium: 610mg,Carbohydrates: 55.

Citrus Fennel And Mint Salad

Servings:2 | Cooking Time:x

Ingredients:
- 1 large navel orange, peeled and sectioned
- 1 cup fennel bulb slices
- 1 medium carrot, peeled and shaved
- 2 radishes, finely sliced
- 2 tablespoons coarsely chopped fresh mint leaves
- 2 tablespoons extra-virgin olive oil
- 1 tablespoon lime juice
- 1/8 teaspoon Himalayan salt
- 1/4 teaspoon freshly ground black pepper

Directions:
1. Add orange to a medium serving bowl.
2. Add fennel, carrot, and radishes to bowl.
3. Add mint to a small bowl with oil, lime juice, salt, and pepper. Whisk well to combine. Pour into serving bowl with rest of ingredients and toss to combine.

Nutrition Info:
- Calories: 185,Fat: 14g,Protein: 2g,Sodium: 197mg,Carbohydrates: 16.

Potato And Corn Chowder

Servings:6 | Cooking Time:x

Ingredients:
- 8 ounces (225 g) lean bacon slices, diced (optional)
- Nonstick cooking spray
- 3 large potatoes, peeled (if desired) and diced
- 8 cups (2 liters) reduced sodium gluten-free, onion-free chicken or vegetable stock*
- One 14.7-ounce (417 g) can no-salt-added, gluten-free cream-style corn
- 1 teaspoon ground mustard
- 1 teaspoon fresh thyme leaves
- 1 heaping tablespoon roughly chopped flat-leaf parsley
- Salt and freshly ground black pepper

Directions:
1. If using the bacon, add to a large heavy-bottomed saucepan over medium heat and cook, stirring, until crisp. Remove to paper towels to drain. Spray the same saucepan with cooking spray, add the potatoes, and cook, still over medium heat, stirring regularly.
2. Pour in the stock and bring to a boil. Reduce the heat to a simmer and cook for 15 minutes, stirring occasionally, until the potatoes are tender.
3. Puree with an immersion blender (or in batches in a regular blender) until smooth. Stir in the corn, mustard, thyme, parsley, and reserved bacon, and season to taste with salt and pepper. Reheat gently without boiling and serve.

Nutrition Info:
- : 283 calories,18 g protein,15 g total fat,18 g carbohydrates,1148 mg sodiu.

Vegan Carrot, Leek, And Saffron Soup

Servings:4 | Cooking Time:x

Ingredients:

- 2 tablespoons butter
- 2 medium leeks, coarsely chopped, leaves only
- 1 medium red bell pepper, seeded and diced
- 1 pound carrots, peeled and sliced
- 1 tablespoon ground coriander
- ¼ teaspoon cayenne pepper
- ½ teaspoon ground turmeric
- ½ teaspoon plus 2 teaspoons saffron
- 4 cups Vegetable Stock (see recipe in this chapter)
- ⅛ teaspoon salt
- ¼ teaspoon white pepper
- ½ cup canned coconut cream or full-fat coconut milk

Directions:

1. Melt butter in a medium saucepan over medium heat. Add leeks and cook 7 minutes or until translucent.
2. Add bell pepper and carrots, and cook another 5–7 minutes or until carrots soften just slightly.
3. Add coriander, cayenne, turmeric, and ½ teaspoon saffron and stir. Cook 1 minute. Add stock, salt, and pepper and bring to a boil. Reduce heat to low and cover. Cook 20–35 minutes or until vegetables are very tender.
4. Remove soup from heat and let cool to room temperature. Using a blender or food processor, purée soup in batches.
5. Serve in soup bowls with a swirl of cream in each and garnished with the remaining saffron.

Nutrition Info:

- Calories: 257,Fat: 12g,Protein: 2g,Sodium: 717mg,Carbohydrates: 37.

Roasted Potato Wedges

Servings:4 | Cooking Time:30 Minutes

Ingredients:

- 1 pound Yukon Gold potatoes, quartered lengthwise
- 2 tablespoons Garlic Oil
- 1 tablespoon chopped fresh rosemary leaves
- ½ teaspoon sea salt
- ¼ teaspoon freshly ground black pepper

Directions:

1. Preheat the oven to 425°F.
2. In a large bowl, toss the potatoes with the garlic oil, rosemary, salt, and pepper. Divide them between two baking sheets and spread into a single layer.
3. Bake for about 30 minutes until the potatoes are browned. Stir them once or twice and rotate the pans (switching racks) halfway through cooking.

Nutrition Info:

- Calories: 143,Total Fat: 7g,Carbohydrates: 19g,Sodium: 241mg,Protein: 2.

Butter Lettuce Salad With Poached Egg And Bacon

Servings:4 | Cooking Time:x

Ingredients:

- 4 slices thick-cut bacon
- 1 tablespoon fresh lemon juice
- 2 teaspoons Dijon mustard
- 2 tablespoons extra-virgin olive oil
- 1/2 teaspoon freshly ground black pepper
- 1 tablespoon rice wine vinegar
- 4 large eggs
- 4 cups butter lettuce

Directions:

1. Preheat oven to 400°F.
2. Line a rimmed baking sheet with parchment paper and place bacon on top of paper. Bake 15–18 minutes or until crisp and browned, rotating baking sheet once. Drain bacon strips on a plate with paper towels. Once cool enough to handle, cut bacon into 1/2" strips.
3. In a small bowl combine lemon juice, mustard, oil, and pepper. Stir well to combine.
4. Pour cold water into a large saucepan until there is at least 4" of water. Add vinegar and bring to a boil over medium heat, then reduce heat to low.
5. Crack 1 egg into a small shallow bowl. Stir water in saucepan continuously to create a whirlpool. Gently pour egg into water. Cook 3–4 minutes until firm. Remove egg from water with a slotted spoon. Skim any remaining foam from water. Repeat with remaining eggs.
6. Place lettuce and bacon in a large salad bowl. Pour in lemon-mustard dressing. Toss well to combine. Divide among 4 plates. Gently add 1 egg to each plate and serve.

Nutrition Info:

- Calories: 223,Fat: 20g,Protein: 9g,Sodium: 324mg,Carbohydrates: 1.

Glorious Strawberry Salad

Servings:4 | Cooking Time:x

Ingredients:

- 6 cups fresh baby spinach
- 1/2 cup sliced strawberries
- 1/4 cup whole walnuts
- 1/4 cup chopped fresh basil
- 1/2 cup crumbled goat cheese
- 1/4 teaspoon sea salt
- 1 tablespoon freshly ground black pepper
- 3 tablespoons rice wine vinegar
- 2/3 cup extra-virgin olive oil
- 1/2 medium avocado, cut into eighths

Directions:

1. In a large salad bowl toss together spinach, strawberries, walnuts, basil, goat cheese, salt, and pepper.
2. In a small bowl whisk together vinegar and oil. Drizzle over salad and toss salad again.
3. Serve on individual salad plates and top each with avocado.

Nutrition Info:

- Calories: 478,Fat: 48g,Protein: 6g,Sodium: 396mg,Carbohydrates: 8.

Roasted Squash And Chestnut Soup

Servings:4 | Cooking Time:x

Ingredients:
- 4½ pounds (2 kg) peeled, seeded, and cubed kabocha or other suitable winter squash
- 2 tablespoons olive oil
- 2 cups (500 g) unsweetened chestnut puree
- 8 cups (2 liters) gluten-free, onion-free chicken or vegetable stock*
- 2 teaspoons ground ginger
- 1 cup (250 ml) low-fat milk, lactose-free milk, or suitable plant-based milk, warmed, plus more for serving (optional)
- Salt and freshly ground black pepper

Directions:
1. Preheat the oven to 350°F (180°C).
2. Spread the squash on a baking sheet and drizzle with the olive oil. Bake, turning occasionally, for 30 to 40 minutes, until golden and cooked through.
3. Transfer the squash to a large saucepan or stockpot. Add the chestnut puree, stock, and ginger and bring to a boil. Reduce the heat and simmer over medium-low heat for 15 to 20 minutes, stirring occasionally, until the squash is tender. Let cool for about 10 minutes.
4. Add the warmed milk to the soup and puree with an immersion blender (or in batches in a regular blender) until smooth. Season to taste with salt and pepper. Finish with a swirl of extra milk (if desired) and serve.

Nutrition Info:
- : 466 calories,9 g protein,10 g total fat,92 g carbohydrates,928 mg sodiu.

Acorn Squash And Chard Soup

Servings:4 | Cooking Time:x

Ingredients:
- 2 medium acorn squash
- 2 tablespoons extra-virgin olive oil, divided
- 1 (6-ounce) package Canadian bacon, diced
- 1 bunch Swiss chard, stems removed, chopped roughly
- 3 cups filtered water
- 1 teaspoon ground turmeric
- 1 teaspoon ground cinnamon
- ¼ teaspoon freshly ground black pepper

Directions:
1. Heat oven to 400ºF. Roast whole squash on a rimmed baking sheet for 1 hour until tender, turning occasionally. Remove from heat and cool for 30 minutes.
2. While squash is cooking, heat 1 tablespoon olive oil over medium heat in a stockpot. Sauté Canadian bacon, stirring occasionally, 8 minutes until browned. Remove from pan using a slotted spoon, leaving drippings in pan, and place on a paper towel–lined plate to dry.
3. Add remaining olive oil to pot. Sauté Swiss chard for 3 minutes, stirring occasionally until wilted.
4. Once squash has cooled, cut each one in half length-wise. Scoop out seeds and discard. Scoop cooked flesh from skin and process in a blender or food processor until smooth.
5. Add puréed squash to soup pot with the chard. Add 3 cups filtered water, turmeric, cinnamon, and pepper. Simmer 5 minutes, uncovered. Remove from heat.
6. Serve with Canadian bacon as garnish.

Nutrition Info:
- Calories: 222,Fat: 10g,Protein: 11g,Sodium: 675mg,Carbohydrates: 25.

Chopped Italian Salad

Servings:4 | Cooking Time:0 Minutes

Ingredients:
- 4 cups chopped romaine lettuce
- 8 cherry tomatoes, halved
- 1 medium zucchini, chopped
- 1 cup black olives, halved
- ¼ cup Italian Balsamic Vinaigrette

Directions:
1. In a medium bowl, combine the lettuce, tomatoes, zucchini, and olives.
2. Add the vinaigrette and toss to coat.

Nutrition Info:
- Calories: 158,Total Fat: 10g,Carbohydrates: 16g,Sodium: 433mg,Protein: 3.

Philly Steak Sandwich

Servings:2 | Cooking Time:15 Minutes

Ingredients:
- 2 tablespoons Garlic Oil
- 1 green bell pepper, sliced
- 1 red bell pepper, sliced
- 6 scallions, green parts only, sliced
- 6 ounces thinly sliced deli roast beef, chopped
- 2 slices gluten-free sandwich bread, toasted
- ½ cup grated Monterey Jack cheese

Directions:
1. In a large nonstick skillet over medium-high heat, heat the garlic oil until it shimmers.
2. Add the green and red bell peppers and the scallions. Cook for about 7 minutes, stirring occasionally, until soft.
3. Add the roast beef, and cook for about 3 minutes more, until the beef is warmed through.
4. Preheat the broiler to high and adjust a rack to the top position.
5. Place the toasted bread on a baking sheet and top each with half the bell peppers and beef.
6. Sprinkle each with ¼ cup grated cheese.
7. Broil for about 3 minutes, until the cheese melts.

Nutrition Info:
- Calories: 501,Total Fat: 31g,Carbohydrates: 30g,Sodium: 641mg,Protein: 28.

Rice Paper "spring Rolls" With Satay Sauce

Servings: 3 (4 Rolls Per Serving) | Cooking Time:30 Minutes

Ingredients:

- Satay sauce
- 4 tbsp peanut butter
- 2 tbsp lemon juice
- 2 tbsp water
- 2 tsp brown sugar
- 1 tsp white sugar
- Rice spring rolls
- 12 rice paper wrappers
- 1 cucumber, small
- 1 carrot, large, cut into matchstick pieces
- 1 cup red cabbage, sliced finely
- ½ cup mint, fresh, chopped roughly
- ½ cup cilantro, fresh, roughly cut

Directions:

1. Prepare the satay sauce first. Soften the peanut butter in a microwaveable bowl for about 30 seconds. Place the rest of the sauce ingredients into the bowl and use a fork to mix until smooth. Add a tbsp of water if the mixture is too thick.
2. Put warm water into a large bowl. One at a time, dip a rice wrapper into the water until it softens slightly then place it on a clean, damp cloth.
3. Place a small amount of the fresh vegetables and herbs onto the bottom third of the wrapper. Do not overfill as it will affect the rolling process.
4. To roll, first, fold the small sides up like a burrito. Next, pull the bottom of the wrapper up gently over the filling. It is best to hold the end with the filling in it in your hands.
5. The rolls are best when dipped in the satay sauce.

Nutrition Info:

- 472g Cal,23.5 g Fat ,48.2 g Carbs ,24.4 g Protein.

Easy Onion- And Garlic-free Chicken Stock

Servings:2 | Cooking Time:x

Ingredients:

- 1 (2-pound) ready-made rotisserie chicken
- 2 quarts cold water
- 2 medium carrots, peeled and cut into chunks
- 1 medium stalk celery with leaves, cut into chunks
- 1 large bok choy stalk with leaves, cut into chunks
- 1/2 teaspoon dried or fresh rosemary
- 1/2 teaspoon dried or fresh thyme
- 4–5 sprigs fresh parsley
- 2 dried bay leaves
- 8 whole peppercorns

Directions:

1. Remove meat from rotisserie chicken and set aside to use for sandwiches, stir-fry, chicken salad, or other recipes.
2. Place chicken carcass in a 4- to 6-quart slow cooker and make sure it is fully covered with water.
3. Place vegetables and spices in slow cooker.
4. Set slow cooker to low and cook 6–8 hours.
5. Use tongs to transfer and discard chicken bones from slow cooker. Place a large sieve over a large bowl. Drain contents from slow cooker through sieve. Discard large vegetable pieces. Skim fat from surface of stock using a large spoon.
6. Cool completely, divide into a few small glass jars or plastic containers, and refrigerate up to 1 week or freeze up to 3 months.

Nutrition Info:

- Calories: 566,Fat: 14g,Protein: 96g,Sodium: 437mg,Carbohydrates: 7.

Roasted Sweet Potato Salad With Spiced Lamb And Spinach

Servings:4 | Cooking Time:x

Ingredients:
- 4 small sweet potatoes, peeled (if desired) and cut into ¾-inch (2 cm) cubes (about 4½ cups/600 g)
- 1 red bell pepper, seeded and cut into quarters
- Olive oil
- 1 heaping tablespoon ground cumin
- 2 teaspoons ground coriander
- ½ teaspoon ground cardamom
- 2 teaspoons ground turmeric
- ½ teaspoon ground sumac, or ½ teaspoon paprika plus ½ teaspoon lemon zest
- 1 pound (450 g) lean lamb steak, cut into thin strips
- 8 ounces (225 g) baby spinach leaves (8 cups), rinsed and dried

Directions:
1. Preheat the oven to 350°F (180°C).
2. Place the sweet potato and bell pepper on a large baking sheet and brush with olive oil. Roast for 30 minutes or until tender and browned. Set aside to cool. When cool enough to handle, remove the skin from the bell pepper.
3. Heat a little olive oil in a medium frying pan over medium-low heat. Add the cumin, coriander, cardamom, turmeric, and sumac and heat for 1 minute or until fragrant. Add the lamb and stir to coat with the spice mix. Cook for 3 to 5 minutes, until just browned. Remove from the heat.
4. Combine the spinach, sweet potato, and bell pepper in a large bowl. Top with the lamb and any pan juices and finish with a drizzle of olive oil.

Nutrition Info:
- : 392 calories,27 g protein,14 g total fat,40 g carbohydrates,171 mg sodiu.

Chicken Noodle Soup With Bok Choy

Servings:4 | Cooking Time:x

Ingredients:
- 8 cups (2 liters) gluten-free, onion-free chicken or vegetable stock*
- 1 heaping tablespoon grated ginger
- 4 kaffir lime leaves
- 1 pound (450 g) boneless, skinless chicken breasts, very thinly sliced
- 8 ounces (225 g) gluten-free rice vermicelli, broken into 2-inch (5 cm) pieces
- 3 bunches baby bok choy, leaves separated, rinsed and drained
- ½ cup (40 g) bean sprouts
- 2 teaspoons gluten-free soy sauce

Directions:
1. Place the stock, ginger, and lime leaves in a large heavy-bottomed saucepan and bring to a boil. Add the chicken, reduce the heat, and simmer for 5 minutes.
2. Add the rice noodles, bok choy, and bean sprouts and simmer for another 5 minutes or until the noodles are tender. Remove the lime leaves, stir in the soy sauce, and serve immediately.

Nutrition Info:
- : 362 calories,31 g protein,2 g total fat,46 g carbohydrates,1023 mg sodiu.

Tomato, Basil, And Olive Risotto

Servings:4 | Cooking Time: 40 Minutes

Ingredients:
- 3 cups homemade (onion- and garlic-free) chicken or vegetable broth
- 3 tablespoons unsalted butter, divided
- 2 tablespoons olive oil
- 1 cup Arborio rice
- 1 (14-ounce) can onion- and garlic-free diced tomatoes, drained
- 6 Kalamata olives, finely chopped
- ½ cup chopped fresh basil
- ¾ cup freshly grated Parmesan cheese

Directions:
1. In a small saucepan, bring the broth to a boil over medium heat. Reduce the heat to low to maintain a gentle simmer.
2. In a large saucepan, heat 1 tablespoon of the butter and the olive oil over medium heat. Add the rice and stir to coat. Add the tomatoes, olives, and about 1 cup of the broth and cook, stirring constantly, until most of the liquid has been absorbed.
3. Continue adding the broth, one ladleful at time, and cook, stirring frequently, until each addition is fully absorbed, about 30 minutes. When all the liquid has been used up and the rice is tender, remove the pan from the heat and stir in the basil, the remaining butter, and the cheese.
4. Cover the risotto and let rest for about 5 minutes. Serve hot, garnished with additional cheese, if desired.

Nutrition Info:
- Calories: 583; Protein: 44g; Total Fat: 26g; Saturated Fat: 12g; Carbohydrates: 43g; Fiber: 3g; Sodium: 456mg;

Kale And Red Bell Pepper Salad

Servings:4 | Cooking Time:0 Minutes

Ingredients:
- 4 cups stemmed, chopped kale, or 1 (9-ounce) bag kale salad
- 1 red bell pepper, stemmed, seeded, and chopped
- ¼ cup pepitas (hulled pumpkin seeds)
- ¼ cup Balsamic Vinaigrette

Directions:
1. In a large bowl, combine the kale, bell pepper, and pepitas.
2. Add the vinaigrette and toss to coat.

Nutrition Info:
- Calories: 149,Total Fat: 10g,Carbohydrates: 12g,Sodium: 151mg,Protein: 4.

Veggie Dip

Servings: 16 | Cooking Time:5 Minutes

Ingredients:

- 1 cup mayonnaise
- 2 cups Greek yogurt
- 2 cups kale, chopped finely
- 1 ½ cups bell peppers, variety of colors, chopped finely
- 2 cups water chestnuts, chopped finely
- 3 spring onions, green parts only, chopped finely
- 1 tsp garlic-infused oil
- Pinch of salt
- Fresh sliced vegetables and corn chips for serving

Directions:

1. In a bowl, mix all the ingredients well, except for the fresh sliced vegetables. Place in the fridge until serving.
2. Serve with the fresh vegetables.

Nutrition Info:

- 123g Cal,10 g Fat ,3 g Carbs ,3 g Protein.

Caprese Salad

Servings:4 | Cooking Time:0 Minutes

Ingredients:

- 2 cups torn romaine lettuce
- 20 cherry tomatoes, quartered
- ¼ cup loosely packed fresh basil leaves, chopped
- 4 ounces mozzarella cheese, chopped
- ¼ cup Italian Basil Vinaigrette

Directions:

1. In a large bowl, combine the lettuce, tomatoes, basil, and cheese.
2. Add the vinaigrette and toss to coat.

Nutrition Info:

- Calories: 265,Total Fat: 14g,Carbohydrates: 26g,Sodium: 202mg,Protein: 14

Cucumber And Sesame Salad

Servings:4 | Cooking Time:0 Minutes

Ingredients:

- 4 medium cucumbers, peeled and chopped
- 6 scallions, green parts only, chopped
- 1 tablespoon sesame seeds
- 1 teaspoon sesame oil
- ¼ cup Cilantro-Lime Vinaigrette

Directions:

1. In a large bowl, combine the cucumbers, scallions, and sesame seeds.
2. In a small bowl, whisk together the sesame oil and vinaigrette. Add the dressing to the cucumber mix and toss to coat.

Nutrition Info:

- Calories: 145,Total Fat: 10g,Carbohydrates: 14g,Sodium: 10mg,Protein: 3.

Bacon Mashed Potatoes

Servings:4 | Cooking Time: 15 Minutes

Ingredients:

- 1 pound new or baby potatoes, cut into 1-inch cubes
- 2 slices bacon
- ⅓ cup lactose-free milk
- ½ teaspoon salt
- ¼ teaspoon freshly ground black pepper
- ¼ cup unsalted butter
- 4 scallions, green parts only, sliced

Directions:

1. Put the potatoes in a large saucepan, cover with 2 inches of water, and bring to a boil over medium-high heat. Lower the heat to medium and cook for 10 to 12 minutes, until the potatoes are tender. Drain the potatoes and place them in a large bowl.
2. While the potatoes are cooking, cook the bacon in a large skillet over medium heat for about 4 minutes per side, until browned and crisp. Drain on paper towels, and then crumble.
3. In the large bowl, mash the potatoes with a potato masher. Add the milk, salt, pepper, and butter. Continue mashing until the potatoes are smooth, the butter is melted, and everything is well mixed. Stir in the bacon and scallions. Serve immediately.

Nutrition Info:

- Calories: 203; Protein: 5g; Total Fat: 14g; Saturated Fat: 8g; Carbohydrates: 16g; Fiber: 3g; Sodium: 479mg;

Lentil Chili

Servings:4 | Cooking Time:x

Ingredients:

- 1 tablespoon olive oil
- 1 medium stalk celery, diced
- 1 large carrot, peeled and diced, or 1 cup store-bought shredded carrots
- 1 large red bell pepper, seeded and chopped
- 4 cups Vegetable Stock (see recipe in this chapter)
- 2 teaspoons chili powder
- 1 teaspoon ground cumin
- 2 cups canned lentils, drained and thoroughly rinsed
- 3 Roma tomatoes, diced
- 1/4 cup chopped fresh cilantro
- 2 cups baby spinach
- 1/2 cup lactose-free sour cream (optional)

Directions:

1. Heat a large pot over medium-high heat and add olive oil.
2. Once hot, add celery, carrot, and bell pepper; sauté about 5 minutes, stirring frequently.
3. Stir in 1/4 cup stock.
4. Add chili powder and cumin and stir; cook 1 minute.
5. Add lentils, tomatoes, cilantro, and remaining stock. Once boiling, reduce heat to medium-low and simmer 25 minutes partially covered.
6. Uncover and cook 8 minutes longer. Add spinach and stir, cooking another 2 minutes.
7. Top with sour cream if using and serve.

Nutrition Info:

- Calories: 236,Fat: 8g,Protein: 12g,Sodium: 614mg,Carbohydrates: 32.

Chicken And Dumplings Soup

Servings:6 | Cooking Time:x

Ingredients:

- 1 whole (3-pound) chicken
- 2 bay leaves
- 6–8 cups water
- 2 tablespoons garlic-infused olive oil
- 5 large carrots, peeled and sliced
- 2 medium stalks celery, sliced
- 1 teaspoon dried thyme
- 1/4 teaspoon salt
- 3 whole peppercorns
- 2 cups gluten-free all-purpose flour
- 1/4 teaspoon xanthan gum
- 2 teaspoons gluten-free baking powder
- 1 teaspoon plus 1 tablespoon finely chopped fresh flat-leaf parsley, divided
- 3/4 teaspoon salt
- 2 large eggs, beaten
- 2 tablespoons butter, melted
- 3/4 cup plus 2 tablespoons lactose-free milk

Directions:

1. Put whole chicken in a large pot and add bay leaves and 6–8 cups water, or enough to cover chicken. Bring to a boil and then simmer with lid on about 1 hour, skimming off any foam. After 1 hour, remove chicken and allow to cool. Keep remaining broth in pot. Once chicken is cool, peel off skin and tear meat off bones. Set meat aside.
2. Heat oil in a large saucepan and sauté carrots and celery 5 minutes.
3. Drain broth from chicken pot through a colander into another large pot or a bowl. Discard any remaining bones and bay leaves and add drained broth to pan with vegetables and add in thyme, salt, and peppercorns. Bring to a simmer.
4. To make dumplings: combine flour, xanthan gum, baking powder, 1 teaspoon parsley, and salt in a medium bowl. Add beaten eggs, butter, and milk; gently mix to combine with a spoon. Mix just until mixture comes together nicely and stays moist. (Overmixing may make dumplings too dense.)
5. Using a soupspoon, spoon out even-sized portions of dough and drop into soup. Cover soup and simmer 20 minutes.
6. Garnish with 1 tablespoon parsley and serve.

Nutrition Info:

- Calories: 530,Fat: 14g,Protein: 56g,Sodium: 856mg,Carbohydrates: 41.

Sauces, Dressings, And Condiments

Sauces, Dressings, And Condiments

Pumpkin Seed Dressing

Servings:1 | Cooking Time:x

Ingredients:
- 1/4 cup hulled green pumpkin seeds
- 1/16 teaspoon wheat-free asafetida powder
- 1/8 cup extra-virgin olive oil
- 1/8 cup water
- 1 tablespoon fresh lemon juice
- 1/4 teaspoon salt
- 1 tablespoon finely chopped fresh cilantro

Directions:
1. Toast pumpkin seeds in a small skillet over medium heat, stirring frequently until just about browned, about 5 minutes.
2. Transfer to a plate to cool 2–3 minutes.
3. Purée seeds in a blender with remaining ingredients. Blend until smooth. Store in an air-tight container in refrigerator for 1–2 weeks.

Nutrition Info:
- Calories: 109,Fat: 11g,Protein: 3g,Sodium: 157mg,Carbohydrates: 1.

Sweet Chili Garlic Sauce

Servings:21 | Cooking Time:x

Ingredients:
- 1 pound fresh chili peppers, ends trimmed
- 1/16 teaspoon wheat-free asafetida powder
- 2 tablespoons safflower oil or other cooking oil
- 1/4 cup rice wine vinegar
- 1/4 cup brown sugar
- 1/4 cup gluten-free fish sauce

Directions:
1. In a food processor add in chili peppers and asafetida powder. Process until minced.
2. In a medium sauté pan heat oil until shimmering on medium-high heat. Add in chili pepper mixture and cook 1 minute. Add in vinegar, sugar, and fish sauce and stir to combine. Turn heat to low and cook 25 minutes.
3. Before removing from heat taste sauce to see if you'd like it sweeter (add 1 tablespoon or more of brown sugar), saltier (add 1 tablespoon or more of fish sauce) or tangier (add 1 tablespoon or more of vinegar). Pour in an air-tight container or canning jar and store in pantry for 1 month or in refrigerator for up to 6 months.

Nutrition Info:
- Calories: 133,Fat: 6g,Protein: 2g,Sodium: 1,129mg,Carbohydrates: 19.

Steakhouse Rub

Servings:4 | Cooking Time:x

Ingredients:
- 1 teaspoon sea salt
- 1/4 teaspoon freshly ground black pepper
- 1/4 teaspoon ground mustard
- 1/2 teaspoon dried thyme
- 1/2 teaspoon dried rosemary, crumbled
- 1/4 teaspoon maple sugar
- 1/2 teaspoon orange zest

Directions:
1. Combine all ingredients in a small bowl.

Nutrition Info:
- Calories: 2,Fat: 0g,Protein: 0g,Sodium: 590mg,Carbohydrates: 0.

Homemade Barbecue Sauce

Servings:1 | Cooking Time: 10 Minutes

Ingredients:

- 6 scallions, green parts only, minced
- ½ cup apple cider vinegar
- 2 tablespoons Garlic Oil
- 2 tablespoons tomato paste
- 1 teaspoon liquid smoke
- 1 packet stevia
- 1 teaspoon chili powder
- ½ teaspoon sea salt
- ⅛ teaspoon freshly ground black pepper

Directions:

1. In a small saucepan over medium heat, combine all the ingredients.
2. Simmer for 5 minutes, stirring. Refrigerate any leftovers for up to 5 days.

Nutrition Info:

- Calories:41; Total Fat: 4g; Saturated Fat: 0g; Carbohydrates: 2g; Fiber: <1g; Sodium: 127mg; Protein: <1g

Sun-dried Tomato Pesto

Servings:1 | Cooking Time:x

Ingredients:

- 2 tablespoons walnut oil
- ¼ cup walnuts, toasted
- ¼ cup sun-dried tomatoes
- 1 cup packed baby spinach leaves
- ½ teaspoon sea salt
- ¼ cup freshly grated Parmesan cheese

Directions:

1. Add all ingredients to a food processor and blend to a pesto consistency.

Nutrition Info:

- Calories: 290,Fat: 27g,Protein: 9g,Sodium: 670mg,Carbohydrates: 7.

Bolognese Sauce

Servings:8 | Cooking Time:x

Ingredients:

- 2 tablespoons extra-virgin olive oil
- 2 tablespoons butter
- 1 medium yellow onion, peeled and quartered
- 2 garlic cloves, peeled, slightly smashed
- 1½ cups finely diced carrots
- 1 pound ground meatball mix (beef, pork, and veal)
- ½ cup dry white wine
- 1 teaspoon sea salt
- ⅛ teaspoon freshly ground black pepper
- ⅛ teaspoon ground nutmeg
- 1 (14.5-ounce) can diced fire-roasted tomatoes
- 1 tablespoon Tomato Paste (see recipe in this chapter)
- 1 (1" × 3") Parmesan cheese rind
- ½ cup Whipped Cream (see recipe in Chapter 14)

Directions:

1. Heat oil and butter over medium-low heat in a large stockpot. Add the onion and garlic and sauté, stirring constantly, until garlic is softened and brown at edges. Remove and discard onion and garlic, leaving oil and butter.
2. Add carrots to oil and sauté over medium-low heat for 15 minutes, stirring occasionally.
3. Add meat and cook, stirring often to break up into bits, for about 10–15 minutes or until meat is fully browned.
4. Add wine and simmer uncovered 10 minutes.
5. Add salt, pepper, nutmeg, tomatoes, paste, and rind, and simmer uncovered 1½–2 hours more, stirring occasionally.
6. Remove rind, fold in whipped cream, and serve.

Nutrition Info:

- Calories: 210,Fat: 14g,Protein: 12g,Sodium: 415mg,Carbohydrates: 6.

Ginger Sesame Salad Dressing

Servings:1 | Cooking Time:x

Ingredients:
- 1/2 cup extra-virgin olive oil
- 1/4 cup rice wine vinegar
- 2 tablespoons gluten-free soy sauce (tamari)
- 2 tablespoons demerara sugar
- 1 teaspoon sesame oil
- 1" piece fresh gingerroot, minced

Directions:

1. Blend all ingredients in a blender or food processor until smooth. Dressing can be stored 1 week in refrigerator. Bring to room temperature before serving.

Nutrition Info:
- Calories: 141,Fat: 14g,Protein: 0g,Sodium: 226mg,Carbohydrates: 4.

Pork Loin Rub

Servings:1 | Cooking Time:x

Ingredients:
- 1 tablespoon sea salt
- 1 tablespoon demerara sugar
- 1 tablespoon ground cinnamon
- 1 tablespoon sweet paprika
- 1 teaspoon dried oregano
- 1/2 teaspoon ground cumin
- 1/2 teaspoon ground red pepper

Directions:

1. Mix all ingredients together in a small bowl.

Nutrition Info:
- Calories: 19,Fat: 0g,Protein: 0g,Sodium: 1,410mg,Carbohydrates: 5.

Olive Tapenade

Servings:1 | Cooking Time: 0 Minutes

Ingredients:
- 1 cup chopped black olives
- 2 tablespoons Garlic Oil
- 2 tablespoons chopped fresh basil leaves
- 1 anchovy fillet, minced
- 1 tablespoon capers, chopped
- Juice of 1/2 lemon
- 1/2 teaspoon sea salt
- 1/8 teaspoon freshly ground black pepper

Directions:

1. In a small bowl, stir together all the ingredients until well mixed.

Nutrition Info:
- Calories:61; Total Fat: 6g; Saturated Fat: <1g; Carbohydrates: 2g; Fiber: <1g; Sodium: 388mg; Protein: <1g

Low-fodmap Spicy Ketchup

Servings:1 | Cooking Time: 20 Minutes

Ingredients:

- 2 tablespoons Garlic Oil (here)
- ¼ cup tomato paste
- ¼ cup light-brown sugar
- ½ teaspoon ground ginger
- ¼ teaspoon cayenne
- ¼ teaspoon ground allspice
- ⅛ teaspoon ground cinnamon
- ⅛ teaspoon ground cloves
- ¼ cup red-wine vinegar
- 1 (15-ounce) can tomato sauce
- ½ teaspoon salt
- ¼ teaspoon freshly ground black pepper

Directions:

1. Heat the Garlic Oil in a small saucepan over medium heat. Add the tomato paste and cook, stirring, for 1 minute.
2. Add the sugar, ginger, cayenne, allspice, cinnamon, and cloves, and cook, stirring frequently, until the sugar is fully dissolved. Stir in the vinegar, tomato sauce, salt, and pepper. Cook, stirring occasionally, for 15 to 20 minutes, until the sauce is very thick.
3. Let cool to room temperature. Serve immediately or store in a covered container in the refrigerator for up to a week.

Nutrition Info:

- Calories: 28; Protein: 1g; Total Fat: 0g; Saturated Fat: 0g; Carbohydrates: 7g; Fiber: 1g; Sodium: 289mg;

Low-fodmap Mayonnaise

Servings:1 | Cooking Time: 0 Minutes

Ingredients:

- 1 egg yolk
- 1 tablespoon red wine vinegar
- ½ teaspoon Dijon mustard
- ¼ teaspoon sea salt
- ¾ cup extra-virgin olive oil

Directions:

1. In a blender or food processor, combine the egg yolk, vinegar, mustard, and salt. Process for about 30 seconds until well combined. With a rubber spatula, scrape down the sides of the blender jar or food processor bowl.
2. Turn the blender or processor to medium speed. Very slowly, drip in the olive oil, 1 drop at a time as the processor or blender runs. After about 10 drops, leave the blender or processor running, then add the rest of the olive oil in a thin stream until it is incorporated and emulsified.
3. The mayo will keep refrigerated for up to 5 days.

Nutrition Info:

- Calories:169; Total Fat: 20g; Saturated Fat: 3g; Carbohydrates: <1g; Fiber: 0g; Sodium: 63mg; Protein: <1g

Tangy Lemon Curd

Servings:2 | Cooking Time: 10 Minutes

Ingredients:
- 1 cup granulated sugar
- 1 tablespoon finely grated lemon zest
- 1 cup lemon juice (from about 5 large lemons)
- 3 tablespoons chilled butter
- 3 eggs, lightly beaten

Directions:

1. In a medium saucepan over medium heat, whisk together the sugar, lemon zest, and lemon juice. Whisk in the butter and eggs, and cook the mixture, stirring constantly (be careful not to let it come to a boil), until it becomes thick, for 8 to 10 minutes.

2. Transfer the mixture to a ramekin or custard bowl, and cover with plastic wrap, pressing the plastic directly onto the surface of the curd to prevent a skin from forming, and chill for 4 hours.

Nutrition Info:
- Calories: 240; Protein: 3g; Total Fat: 12.4g; Saturated Fat: 7.2g; Carbohydrates: 32g; Fiber: 2g; Sodium: 42mg;

Basil Sauce

Servings:1 | Cooking Time:x

Ingredients:
- ¼ cup tahini
- ¼ cup fresh flat-leaf parsley leaves
- ¼ cup coarsely chopped fresh chives
- 1 packed cup fresh basil
- Juice of 2 medium lemons
- ¼ cup olive oil
- ¼ teaspoon sea salt
- ¼ teaspoon freshly ground black pepper

Directions:

1. Add all ingredients to a food processor. Blend until smooth. Store in an air-tight container in refrigerator for 5–7 days or in freezer for 3–4 months.

Nutrition Info:
- Calories: 56,Fat: 5g,Protein: 1g,Sodium: 42mg,Carbohydrates: 2.

Garlic-infused Oil

Servings:1 | Cooking Time:x

Ingredients:
- 1 cup plus 1 teaspoon grapeseed oil
- 4 garlic cloves, peeled, slightly smashed

Directions:

1. Heat oil in a small saucepan over medium-low heat, add garlic, and sauté for 10 minutes, stirring often. Remove from heat and allow to completely cool. Remove and discard garlic, reserving oil.

Nutrition Info:
- Calories: 123,Fat: 14g,Protein: 0g,Sodium: 0mg,Carbohydrates: 0.

Roasted Tomato Sauce

Servings:2 | Cooking Time:x

Ingredients:
- 2 tablespoons Garlic-Infused Oil (see recipe in this chapter)
- 1 teaspoon salt
- 1 1/2 pounds fresh tomatoes, cored, seeded and diced
- 1 bay leaf
- 1/8 teaspoon crushed red pepper

Directions:
1. Preheat oven to 400°F. Line a roasting pan with parchment paper.
2. Place all ingredients in a medium bowl and toss to thoroughly combine. Transfer to roasting pan and spread tomatoes in one thin layer.
3. Roast for 20 minutes, tossing halfway through. Remove and discard bay leaf. Transfer to a bowl and stir.

Nutrition Info:
- Calories: 90,Fat: 7g,Protein: 1g,Sodium: 600mg,Carbohydrates: 7.

Artisanal Ketchup

Servings:3 | Cooking Time:x

Ingredients:
- 3/4 cup Tomato Paste (see recipe in this chapter)
- 1 tablespoon white wine vinegar
- 1 tablespoon Simple Brown Syrup (see recipe in Chapter 16)
- 1/4 teaspoon dried oregano
- 1/8 teaspoon ground cumin
- 1/8 teaspoon ground cinnamon
- Water (as needed)

Directions:
1. Blend all ingredients in a food processor, adding water 1/4 cup at a time, until desired consistency is achieved.

Nutrition Info:
- Calories: 53,Fat: 2g,Protein: 1g,Sodium: 55mg,Carbohydrates: 8.

Cilantro-coconut Pesto

Servings:1 | Cooking Time: None

Ingredients:
- 1 bunch cilantro
- 6 tablespoons unsweetened shredded coconut
- 6 tablespoons toasted peanuts
- 1/2 jalapeño, serrano, or Thai chile (optional)
- Juice of 1/2 lemon
- 1 tablespoon Garlic Oil (here)
- 1 tablespoon olive oil
- Salt to taste

Directions:
1. In a food processor, roughly chop the cilantro. Add the coconut, peanuts, chile (if using), and lemon juice, and process to a paste.
2. With the processor running, add the Garlic Oil and olive oil, and process until the desired texture has been achieved. If the mixture is too thick, add more oil or lemon juice or a bit of water. Taste and add salt as needed.

Nutrition Info:
- Calories: 90; Protein: 2g; Total Fat: 8g; Saturated Fat: 3g; Carbohydrates: 3g; Fiber: 1g; Sodium: 23mg;

Sweet-and-sour Sauce

Servings:1 | Cooking Time: 5 Minutes

Ingredients:
- ½ cup pineapple juice
- ⅓ cup rice vinegar
- ¼ cup packed brown sugar
- ¼ cup tomato sauce
- 1 tablespoon gluten-free soy sauce
- 1 tablespoon cornstarch

Directions:
1. In a small saucepan over medium-high heat, whisk together all the ingredients.
2. Simmer for about 5 minutes, whisking, until the sauce thickens.

Nutrition Info:
- Calories:39; Total Fat: 0g; Saturated Fat: 0g; Carbohydrates: 8g; Fiber: 0g; Sodium: 155mg; Protein: <1g

Garlic Oil

Servings:1 | Cooking Time: 5 Minutes

Ingredients:
- 1 cup olive oil
- 6 cloves garlic, sliced

Directions:
1. Heat the olive oil in a small saucepan over medium-low heat.
2. Add the garlic and cook at a low simmer, stirring often, for 5 minutes.
3. Strain the oil through a fine-meshed sieve and discard the solids.
4. Refrigerate the oil in a covered container for up to a week.

Nutrition Info:
- Calories: 108; Protein: 0g; Total Fat: 13g; Saturated Fat: 2g; Carbohydrates: 0g; Fiber: 0g; Sodium: 0mg;

Sun-dried Tomato Spread

Servings:x | Cooking Time:x

Ingredients:
- 1 cup (150 g) sun-dried tomatoes in oil, drained and roughly chopped (oil reserved)
- ¼ cup (15 g) roughly chopped flat-leaf parsley
- 2 heaping tablespoons reduced-fat cream cheese, at room temperature
- 1 tablespoon garlic-infused olive oil
- 3 tablespoons olive oil
- Salt and freshly ground black pepper

Directions:
1. Place the sun-dried tomatoes and reserved oil, parsley, and cream cheese in a food processor or blender and process until well combined.
2. Gradually add the garlic-infused oil and olive oil until the mixture is almost smooth.
3. Season to taste with salt and pepper.
4. Spoon into a bowl or jar, cover, and store in the fridge for up to 3 days.

Nutrition Info:
- 134 calories; 1 g protein; 13 g total fat; 3 g saturated fat; 3 g carbohydrates; 1 g fiber; 122 mg sodium

Basic Marinara Sauce

Servings:41 | Cooking Time:x

Ingredients:

- 16 Roma tomatoes, chopped, or 1 (35-ounce) can San Marzano tomatoes
- 1 tablespoon garlic-infused olive oil
- 1 tablespoon plus 2 teaspoons extra-virgin olive oil
- 1/4 teaspoon of red pepper flakes
- 1 teaspoon salt
- 20 leaves fresh basil, chopped

Directions:

1. Add tomatoes to a large mixing bowl. Using your hands or a potato masher, crush the tomatoes and break up into small pieces.
2. Heat a 2-quart pot on medium-high. Pour both oils into pot and stir with red pepper flakes. Wait 1 minute and then add crushed tomatoes; stir well.
3. Increase heat to high and sprinkle in salt. Add basil and stir to combine.
4. Bring sauce to a boil and cover. Reduce heat to medium-high and cook 10–12 minutes, keeping sauce at a rolling simmer.
5. Uncover and cook another 5 minutes. Remove from heat. Use immediately or transfer to an airtight container and store in refrigerator for 3–4 days or in freezer for 5–6 months.

Nutrition Info:

- Calories: 59,Fat: 5g,Protein: 1g,Sodium: 283mg,Carbohydrates: 5.

Raspberry Lemon Chia Seed Jam

Servings:1 | Cooking Time:x

Ingredients:

- 1/2 pint (or 6 ounces) fresh raspberries
- 1 tablespoon lemon juice
- 1 tablespoon lemon zest
- 2 1/2 tablespoons pure maple syrup
- 1 tablespoon chia seeds

Directions:

1. Add fruit, lemon juice, lemon zest, and maple syrup to a small saucepan and cook over medium-high heat. Cover. Stir occasionally until fruit begins to thicken, about 10 minutes.
2. Uncover and bring mixture to a boil until it develops a sauce-like consistency, about 5 minutes.
3. Stir in chia seeds and cook 2 more minutes. Stir again and then remove from heat.
4. Transfer jam to an airtight jar or other container and allow to cool, or refrigerate 2–3 hours before use. The jam will continue to thicken. Can be stored in refrigerator 2 weeks or frozen up to 2 months.

Nutrition Info:

- Calories: 32,Fat: 1g,Protein: 1g,Sodium: 1mg,Carbohydrates: 7.

Maple Mustard Dipping Sauce

Servings:4 | Cooking Time:x

Ingredients:

- 1 tablespoon light sour cream
- 1 tablespoon pure maple syrup
- 1 tablespoon Dijon mustard

Directions:

1. Whisk together all ingredients in a small bowl and serve.

Nutrition Info:

- Calories: 20,Fat: 0g,Protein: 0g,Sodium: 45mg,Carbohydrates: 4.

Garden Pesto

Servings:1 | Cooking Time:x

Ingredients:
- 2 tablespoons Garlic-Infused Oil (see recipe in this chapter)
- 1/4 cup pine nuts, toasted
- 1 cup packed basil leaves
- 1/2 teaspoon sea salt
- 1/4 cup freshly grated Parmesan cheese

Directions:
1. Add all ingredients to a food processor and blend to a pesto consistency.

Nutrition Info:
- Calories: 178,Fat: 17g,Protein: 5g,Sodium: 350mg,Carbohydrates: 2.

Caesar Salad Dressing

Servings:11 | Cooking Time:x

Ingredients:
- 6 anchovy fillets packed in oil, drained and chopped
- 1/16 teaspoon wheat-free asafetida powder
- 2 large egg yolks
- 2 tablespoons fresh lemon juice
- 3/4 teaspoon Dijon mustard
- 2 tablespoons garlic-infused olive oil
- 1/2 cup extra virgin olive oil
- 3 tablespoons finely grated Parmesan cheese
- 1/4 teaspoon kosher salt
- 1 teaspoon freshly ground black pepper

Directions:
1. In a small bowl, mash anchovies and asafetida into a paste, then place in a medium bowl.
2. Whisk in egg yolks, lemon juice, and mustard. Slowly whisk in garlic-infused oil and then olive oil.
3. Whisk in Parmesan, salt, and pepper. Store in an air-tight container in refrigerator for 3–4 days.

Nutrition Info:
- Calories: 74,Fat: 7g,Protein: 3g,Sodium: 306mg,Carbohydrates: 1.

Pepperonata Sauce

Servings:8 | Cooking Time:x

Ingredients:
- 2 tablespoons Garlic-Infused Oil (see recipe in this chapter)
- 12 medium red, yellow, and green bell peppers, seeded and diced
- 1 tablespoon balsamic vinegar
- 1/8 teaspoon sea salt
- 1/8 teaspoon freshly ground pepper

Directions:
1. Heat oil over medium heat in a large stockpot. Add peppers and sauté 5 minutes. Add vinegar, salt, and pepper and stir.
2. Reduce heat and simmer uncovered for 11/2–2 hours, stirring occasionally, until peppers are fork tender.

Nutrition Info:
- Calories: 87,Fat: 4g,Protein: 2g,Sodium: 45mg,Carbohydrates: 11.

Snacks & Desserts

The Balanced Low-FODMAP Diet
Cookbook for Beginners

Snacks & Desserts

Lemon Cheesecake

Servings:10 | Cooking Time:x

Ingredients:

- 9 ounces (250 g) gluten-free vanilla cookies, crushed (about 2½ cups)
- 4 tablespoons (½ stick/60 g) unsalted butter, melted
- 1 heaping tablespoon unflavored gelatin powder
- One 8-ounce (225 g) package reduced-fat cream cheese, at room temperature
- ¾ cup (165 g) superfine sugar
- 2 tablespoons plus 2 teaspoons fresh lemon juice
- 1 to 2 heaping tablespoons grated lemon zest

- 1⅓ cups (300 ml) light whipping cream
- 1½ teaspoons unflavored gelatin powder
- 3 tablespoons (45 g) unsalted butter, cut into cubes, at room temperature
- ½ cup (110 g) superfine sugar
- 1 large egg yolk, lightly beaten
- 1 teaspoon grated lemon zest
- 2 tablespoons plus 2 teaspoons fresh lemon juice

Directions:

1. Mix together the crushed cookies and melted butter in a medium bowl. Press evenly into the bottom of an 8-inch (20 cm) springform pan. Refrigerate while you prepare the filling and topping.

2. To make the filling, add ½ cup (125 ml) cold water to a small heatproof bowl and whisk in the gelatin with a fork. Set aside for 5 minutes, or until the gelatin has begun to gel. Fill a larger bowl with boiling water, set the bowl containing the gelatin into it, and stir constantly until the gelatin has completely dissolved.

3. Combine the cream cheese, sugar, lemon juice, lemon zest, and dissolved gelatin in a food processor or blender and process for 1 to 2 minutes, until smooth.

4. Beat the cream in a medium bowl with a handheld electric mixer until thickened. Using a large metal spoon, fold the whipped cream into the cream cheese mixture. Pour the filling into the cookie crust. Cover and refrigerate for 3 hours, until set.

5. To make the topping, add ½ cup (125 ml) cold water to a small heatproof bowl and whisk in the gelatin with a fork. Set aside for 5 minutes, until the gelatin has begun to gel. Fill a larger bowl with boiling water, set the bowl containing the gelatin in it, and stir constantly until the gelatin has completely dissolved.

6. Combine the dissolved gelatin, butter, sugar, egg yolk, and lemon zest and juice in a small saucepan. Stir over low heat for about 15 minutes, until thick enough to coat the back of a spoon. Let cool to room temperature.

7. Pour the topping evenly over the filling, then return the cheesecake to the refrigerator for at least 3 hours, until set.

Nutrition Info:

- 380 calories; 7 g protein; 24 g total fat; 12 g saturated fat; 37 g carbohydrates; 1 g fiber; 160 mg sodium

Lamb Meatballs

Servings:4 | Cooking Time: 20 Minutes

Ingredients:
- Oil for preparing the pan
- 1 pound ground lamb
- ½ cup cooked rice
- ⅓ cup crumbled feta cheese
- Zest of 1 lemon
- 3 tablespoons minced parsley
- 1 teaspoon salt
- 1 teaspoon ground cumin
- 1 teaspoon ground allspice
- ½ teaspoon ground cinnamon
- 1 egg, lightly beaten
- 1 tablespoon Garlic Oil (here)

Directions:
1. Preheat the oven to 400°F.
2. Line a large, rimmed baking sheet with lightly oiled parchment paper.
3. In a mixing bowl, combine the lamb, rice, cheese, lemon zest, parsley, salt, cumin, allspice, cinnamon, and egg, and mix well.
4. Form the lamb mixture into 1½-inch balls and arrange them on the prepared baking sheet.
5. Bake the meatballs in the preheated oven until they are browned and cooked through, for about 20 minutes.
6. Drizzle the Garlic Oil over the meatballs just before serving and serve hot.

Nutrition Info:
- Calories: 361; Protein: 37g; Total Fat: 13g; Saturated Fat: 6g; Carbohydrates: 21g; Fiber: 1g; Sodium: 844mg;

Baked Veggie Chips

Servings:6 | Cooking Time: 20 Minutes

Ingredients:
- 2 medium parsnips, peeled
- 2 medium zucchini
- 2 medium carrots, peeled
- Olive oil spray
- 1 teaspoon salt, plus more for garnish

Directions:
1. Using a handheld mandoline or a very sharp knife, slice the vegetables into very thin (1/16-inch) rounds.
2. Preheat the oven to 375°F.
3. Lightly oil 2 large baking sheets with olive oil spray.
4. Arrange the sliced vegetables on paper towels in a single layer, season with 1 teaspoon of salt, and let sit for 15 minutes. Dry the vegetables as thoroughly as possible with a paper towel.
5. Arrange the vegetable slices on the baking sheets in a single layer and coat with additional olive oil spray. Bake in the preheated oven for about 20 minutes.
6. Remove the chips from the oven, sprinkle them with additional salt, and let cool for 5 minutes. Serve immediately or cool to room temperature. The chips can then be stored in a sealed container on the countertop for up to 3 days.

Nutrition Info:
- Calories: 86; Protein: 2g; Total Fat: 1g; Saturated Fat: 0g; Carbohydrates: 20g; Fiber: 6g; Sodium: 417mg;

Low-fodmap Hummus

Servings:4 | Cooking Time: 0 Minutes

Ingredients:
- 1 zucchini
- 2 tablespoons tahini
- 2 tablespoons Garlic Oil
- Juice of 1 lemon
- ½ teaspoon sea salt
- Assorted low-FODMAP veggies, for dipping

Directions:
1. In a blender, combine the zucchini, tahini, garlic oil, lemon juice, and salt. Process until smooth.
2. Serve with the veggies for dipping.

Nutrition Info:
- Calories:116; Total Fat: 11g; Saturated Fat: 2g; Carbohydrates: 4g; Fiber: 1g; Sodium: 251mg; Protein: 2g

Chocolate Lava Cakes

Servings:4 | Cooking Time: 15 Minutes

Ingredients:
- 4 tablespoons unsalted butter, plus more for preparing the ramekins
- 5 ounces dark chocolate, chopped
- 2 eggs
- 2 egg yolks
- ¼ cup granulated sugar
- ½ teaspoon vanilla extract
- 3 tablespoons gluten-free all-purpose flour
- ⅛ teaspoon xanthan gum
- 1 tablespoon unsweetened cocoa powder
- ⅛ teaspoon salt
- Powdered sugar, whipped cream, or Whipped Coconut Cream (here) for serving (optional)

Directions:
1. Preheat the oven to 425°F.
2. Butter the insides of 4 (4-ounce) oven-safe ramekins and place the ramekins in a baking dish.
3. In the top of a double boiler set over simmering water, combine the chocolate and 4 tablespoons butter, stirring frequently, until melted.
4. In a large bowl, whisk together the eggs, egg yolks, sugar, and vanilla until the mixture becomes thick and very pale yellow. While whisking, slowly add the melted chocolate-butter mixture to the egg mixture until well combined.
5. Stir in the flour, xanthan gum, cocoa powder, and salt. Transfer the mixture to the prepared ramekins in the baking dish, dividing equally.
6. Place the baking dish in the preheated oven and add water to the baking dish so that it comes halfway up the sides of the ramekins. Bake for about 15 minutes, until the centers of the cakes are just barely set.
7. Carefully remove the ramekins from the baking dish and transfer them to a wire rack. Cool for about 10 minutes. Before serving, run a butter knife around the edge of each cake to loosen it from the ramekin and then invert it onto a serving plate. Serve immediately, with a dusting of powdered sugar or a dollop of whipped cream or Whipped Coconut Cream.

Nutrition Info:
- Calories: 415; Protein: 7g; Total Fat: 27g; Saturated Fat: 16g; Carbohydrates: 38g; Fiber: 2g; Sodium: 146mg;

Strawberry-rhubarb Crisp With Oat-pecan Topping

Servings:6 | Cooking Time: 40 Minutes

Ingredients:
- FOR THE FILLING
- Butter or coconut oil for preparing the pan
- 2 cups sliced strawberries
- 1 cup finely chopped rhubarb
- ¼ cup sugar
- ⅛ teaspoon salt
- FOR THE TOPPING
- 1 cup gluten-free rolled oats
- ½ cup gluten-free oat flour
- ½ cup roughly chopped pecans
- ¼ cup packed light-brown sugar
- Pinch salt
- 4 tablespoons cold unsalted butter

Directions:
1. Preheat the oven to 350°F.
2. Grease a baking dish or 9-inch pie dish with butter or coconut oil.
3. In a medium bowl, combine the strawberries, rhubarb, sugar, and salt, and stir to mix. Transfer the mixture to the prepared baking dish.
4. To make the topping, combine the oats, oat flour, pecans, brown sugar, and salt in a medium bowl. Add the butter and mix with your hands until the butter is incorporated. Transfer the topping to the dish with the fruit, spreading it in an even layer over the top.
5. Bake in the preheated oven until the top is lightly browned and the filling is bubbly, for 35 to 40 minutes.

Nutrition Info:
- Calories: 277; Protein: 4g; Total Fat: 14g; Saturated Fat: 6g; Carbohydrates: 38g; Fiber: 4g; Sodium: 115mg;

No-bake Coconut Cookie Bars

Servings:12 | Cooking Time: None

Ingredients:
- 2 cups shredded unsweetened coconut
- ½ cup maple syrup
- ¼ cup coconut oil
- 1 teaspoon vanilla extract
- ¼ teaspoon salt

Directions:
1. Combine all of the ingredients in a food processor and process to combine well.
2. Transfer the mixture to a baking dish or rectangular cake pan (8-by-11-inch or similar capacity), and chill in the refrigerator for 1 hour.
3. Cut into 12 bars and serve chilled.

Nutrition Info:
- Calories: 122; Protein: 1g; Total Fat: 9g; Saturated Fat: 8g; Carbohydrates: 11g; Fiber: 1g; Sodium: 54mg;

Lemon Tartlets

Servings:x | Cooking Time:x

Ingredients:
- MAKES 12
- Nonstick cooking spray
- ½ cup (75 g) cornstarch
- 1¼ cups (300 ml) water
- Grated zest of 2 lemons
- ¾ cup (180 ml) fresh lemon juice
- 4 tablespoons (½ stick/60 g) unsalted butter, cut into cubes, at room temperature
- ⅔ cup (150 g) sugar
- 2 large egg yolks
- 1 batch Tart Crust dough, chilled
- Gluten-free, lactose-free ice cream, for serving

Directions:
1. Preheat the oven to 325°F (170°C). Grease twelve tartlet pans or a 12-cup muffin pan with cooking spray.
2. To make the filling, blend the cornstarch with 1 tablespoon of the water in a small saucepan to form a smooth paste. Add the remaining water, stirring to ensure there are no lumps, then add the lemon zest, lemon juice, butter, and sugar and stir over medium-low heat until thickened, 3 to 5 minutes. Remove from the heat and let cool for 10 minutes. Stir in the egg yolks. Pour into a bowl, cover, and refrigerate until cold.
3. Meanwhile, place the chilled dough between two sheets of parchment paper and roll out to a thickness of about ⅛ inch (2 to 3 mm). Cut out 12 rounds with a pastry cutter to fit the pan or cups. Place in the pan or cups and trim the edges to neaten. Bake for 12 to 15 minutes, until golden. Let cool on a wire rack.
4. Spoon the chilled lemon filling into the tartlet crusts and serve with ice cream.

Nutrition Info:
- 297 calories; 4 g protein; 15 g total fat; 9 g saturated fat; 39 g carbohydrates; 1 g fiber; 12 mg sodium

Cinnamon Panna Cotta With Pureed Banana

Servings:4 | Cooking Time:x

Ingredients:
- Nonstick cooking spray
- 1⅔ cups (420 ml) light cream
- ½ cup (125 ml) milk, lactose-free milk, or suitable plant-based milk
- ½ cup (110 g) superfine sugar
- 1 teaspoon ground cinnamon
- 1 teaspoon vanilla extract
- 2¼ teaspoons unflavored gelatin powder
- Ice cubes
- 2 ripe bananas, peeled
- 2 teaspoons light brown sugar

Directions:
1. Grease four 4-ounce (125 ml) dariole molds, custard cups, or tall ramekins with cooking spray.
2. Combine the cream, milk, superfine sugar, cinnamon, and vanilla in a medium saucepan over low heat. Cook, stirring regularly, taking care not to let it boil, for 20 minutes, or until the mixture is thick enough to coat the back of a spoon. Remove from the heat and pour into a medium heatproof bowl.
3. Add 1 tablespoon of cold water to a small heatproof bowl and whisk in the gelatin with a fork. Set it aside for 5 minutes, or until the gelatin has begun to gel. Fill a larger bowl with boiling water, set the bowl containing the gelatin in it, and stir constantly until the gelatin has completely dissolved. Whisk into the cream mixture.
4. Fill a large bowl with ice cubes. Place the bowl with the cream mixture on the ice and whisk every few minutes for about 10 minutes. The mixture will thicken as it cools. When it is thick enough to coat the back of a spoon, carefully pour it into the molds. Refrigerate, covered, for 2 to 3 hours, until set.
5. Combine the bananas and brown sugar in a bowl and mash with a fork until smooth and well combined.
6. To serve, dip each mold in hot water for a few seconds, then turn out onto plates. Spoon the pureed banana into a piping bag and use to decorate the plates (or dollop directly onto the panna cotta, if preferred).

Nutrition Info:
- 370 calories; 5 g protein; 20 g total fat; 12 g saturated fat; 46 g carbohydrates; 2 g fiber; 60 mg sodium

Raspberry–chia Seed Ice Pops

Servings:6 | Cooking Time: None

Ingredients:
- 1½ cup raspberries (fresh or thawed frozen)
- 4 tablespoons sugar, divided
- ½ cup water
- 6 ice-pop molds and handles
- 1 (15-ounce) can light coconut milk
- 1½ tablespoons chia seeds

Directions:
1. In a blender, combine the raspberries, 2 tablespoons of the sugar, and water and blend until smooth.
2. Fill each ice-pop mold with about 1 inch of the raspberry mixture, and place in the freezer to harden (about 30 minutes). Place the remaining raspberry mixture in the refrigerator.
3. Whisk together the coconut milk, the remaining 2 tablespoons sugar, and the chia seeds in a small bowl.
4. Add the coconut milk mixture to the ice-pop molds, distributing evenly. Freeze for another 30 minutes.
5. Add the remaining raspberry mixture to the ice-pop molds, add the sticks or handles, and freeze for at least 4 hours, until completely frozen solid.

Nutrition Info:
- Calories: 115; Protein: 1g; Total Fat: 6g; Saturated Fat: 0g; Carbohydrates: 14g; Fiber: 3g; Sodium: 16mg;

Prosciutto-wrapped Cantaloupe

Servings:4 | Cooking Time: 0 Minutes

Ingredients:
- 8 (½- to 1-inch-thick) cantaloupe wedges, rind removed
- 8 thin prosciutto slices

Directions:
1. Wrap each melon wedge in a slice of prosciutto and secure it with a toothpick.
2. Chill or serve immediately.

Nutrition Info:
- Calories:73; Total Fat: 2g; Saturated Fat: <1g; Carbohydrates: 4g; Fiber: 0g; Sodium: 517mg; Protein: 9g

Deviled Eggs

Servings:6 | Cooking Time: 0 Minutes

Ingredients:
- 6 hardboiled eggs, peeled and halved lengthwise
- ½ cup Low-FODMAP Mayonnaise
- 2 tablespoons Dijon mustard
- 3 scallions, green parts only, minced
- ½ teaspoon sea salt
- ½ teaspoon ground paprika
- ⅛ teaspoon freshly ground black pepper

Directions:
1. Into a small bowl, scoop the egg yolks from the whites. Set the whites aside.
2. Add the mayonnaise, mustard, scallions, salt, paprika, and pepper to the yolks and mash them with a fork.
3. Spoon the mixture back into the egg whites.

Nutrition Info:
- Calories:240; Total Fat: 18g; Saturated Fat: 4g; Carbohydrates: 11g; Fiber: 1g; Sodium: 537mg; Protein: 10g

Quinoa Muffins

Servings:24 | Cooking Time: 20 Minutes

Ingredients:
- 1 ½ cups quinoa flour
- 1 cup quinoa flakes
- ⅓ cup walnuts, chopped
- 1 tbsp cinnamon
- 4 tsp baking powder
- 2 tsp baking soda
- Pinch of salt
- 4 eggs
- 4 bananas, mashed
- ½ cup almond milk
- ¼ cup maple syrup

Directions:
1. Preheat the oven to 375°F.
2. Mix the dry ingredients in one bowl. In a separate bowl, combine the wet ingredients. Combine the ingredients until mixed fully.
3. Spoon into greased muffin pans and bake for 20 minutes. Check if the center is dry by poking the center of a muffin with a skewer. If it comes out clean, they are ready.

Nutrition Info:
- 175g Calories, 10.5g Total fat, 4g Saturated fat, 6g Carbohydrates, 1.5 g Fiber, 14g Protein, 4g Sodium.

Kiwi Yogurt Freezer Bars

Servings:6 | Cooking Time: 0 Minutes

Ingredients:
- Freezing: Overnight
- 2 cups unsweetened almond milk
- 4 kiwis, peeled and chopped
- ½ cup lactose-free plain yogurt
- 4 packets stevia

Directions:
1. In a blender, combine the almond milk, kiwis, yogurt, and stevia. Process until smooth.
2. Pour the mixture into 6 ice pop molds.
3. Refrigerate overnight.

Nutrition Info:
- Calories:59; Total Fat: 2g; Saturated Fat: 0g; Carbohydrates: 10g; Fiber: 2g; Sodium: 76mg; Protein: 2g

Amaretti Tiramisu

Servings:6 | Cooking Time:x

Ingredients:

- 4 large eggs, separated
- ½ cup (110 g) superfine sugar, plus more for the coffee (optional)
- 12 ounces (340 g) reduced-fat cream cheese, at room temperature
- 1 cup (250 ml) strong brewed coffee
- ¼ cup (60 ml) Marsala or amaretto (optional)
- About 30 Amaretti
- ½ teaspoon instant coffee
- ⅔ cup (110 g) confectioners' sugar
- 2 heaping tablespoons unsweetened cocoa powder, plus more for dusting

Directions:

1. Combine the egg yolks and superfine sugar in a large bowl and beat with a handheld electric mixer until thick, pale and creamy. Beat in the cream cheese for 3 to 4 minutes, until the mixture is smooth and well combined.
2. Clean the mixer beaters. Place the egg whites in a large clean bowl and beat until stiff peaks form. Using a large metal spoon, gently fold the egg whites into the cream cheese mixture.
3. Combine the coffee, sugar to taste, and the liqueur (if using) in a small bowl. Dip each Amaretti cookie into the coffee. Place 1 cookie in each of six glass dessert dishes and top with a few tablespoons of the cream cheese filling. Repeat with the remaining cookies and filling, finishing with a cream cheese layer.
4. To make the chocolate sauce, dissolve the instant coffee in 2 to 3 tablespoons hot water. Sift the confectioners' sugar and cocoa into a small bowl, add the coffee mixture, and stir until smooth.
5. Drizzle the chocolate sauce over the tiramisu and dust with additional cocoa. Cover and refrigerate for at least 2 hours, preferably overnight, before serving.

Nutrition Info:

- 415 calories; 13 g protein; 20 g total fat; 8 g saturated fat; 45 g carbohydrates; 2 g fiber; 236 mg sodium

Cucumbers With Cottage Cheese Ranch Dip

Servings:4 | Cooking Time: 0 Minutes

Ingredients:

- ½ cup cottage cheese
- ½ cup Low-FODMAP Mayonnaise
- 6 scallions, green parts only, finely chopped
- 1 teaspoon chopped fresh dill
- Zest of 1 lemon
- ½ teaspoon sea salt
- ¼ teaspoon freshly ground black pepper
- 2 cucumbers, sliced

Directions:

1. In a medium bowl, stir together the cottage cheese, mayonnaise, scallions, dill, lemon zest, salt, and pepper until well mixed.
2. Chill or serve immediately with the cucumber slices.

Nutrition Info:

- Calories:171; Total Fat: 11g; Saturated Fat: 2g; Carbohydrates: 15g; Fiber: 1g; Sodium: 565mg; Protein: 6g

Dairy-free Coffee Ice Cream

Servings:6 | Cooking Time: 5 Minutes

Ingredients:
- 2 (15-ounce) cans full-fat coconut milk
- ¾ cup granulated sugar
- ¾ strong brewed coffee
- 1½ teaspoons vanilla extract

Directions:
1. In a medium saucepan set over medium heat, whisk together the coconut milk, sugar, and coffee, and heat for about 5 minutes, until the sugar is dissolved. Remove from the heat and stir in the vanilla.
2. Transfer to a bowl and chill, covered, in the refrigerator for several hours or overnight.
3. Transfer the mixture to an ice cream maker and freeze according to the manufacturer's instructions.
4. Transfer to a freezer-safe container and freeze for several hours until very firm. Serve frozen.

Nutrition Info:
- Calories: 357; Protein: 2g; Total Fat: 26g; Saturated Fat: 21g; Carbohydrates: 30g; Fiber: 0g; Sodium: 36mg;

Layered Tahitian Lime Cheesecake

Servings:10 | Cooking Time:x

Ingredients:
- 9 ounces (250 g) gluten-free vanilla cookies, crushed (about 2½ cups)
- 4 tablespoons (½ stick/60 g) butter, melted
- 2 tablespoons unflavored gelatin powder
- Two 8-ounce (225 g) packages reduced-fat cream cheese, at room temperature
- One 14-ounce (396 g) can fat free sweetened condensed milk
- ⅓ cup (80 ml) coconut liqueur (see Notes)
- 3 tablespoons plus 1 teaspoon fresh lime juice
- Finely grated zest of 1 lime
- 1 to 2 drops green food coloring

Directions:
1. Mix together the crushed cookies and melted butter in a medium bowl. Press evenly into the bottom of a 9-inch (23 cm) springform pan. Place in the refrigerator while you prepare the topping.
2. Add ½ cup (125 ml) cold water to a small heatproof bowl and whisk in the gelatin with a fork. Set aside for 5 minutes, or until the gelatin has begun to gel. Fill a larger bowl with boiling water, set the bowl containing the gelatin in it, and stir constantly until the gelatin has completely dissolved.
3. Combine the dissolved gelatin, cream cheese, and condensed milk in a food processor or blender and process for 1 minute, or until smooth.
4. Pour half of the mixture into a clean bowl; there should be about 2 cups (500 ml). Add the coconut liqueur to the bowl and mix it in well. Pour over the cookie crust and freeze for 10 minutes.
5. Add the lime juice, lime zest, and food coloring to the remaining batter in the food processor and process for 30 seconds, or until well combined.
6. Remove the cheesecake from the freezer—it should be just set. Pour the lime mixture over the coconut layer, then refrigerate for 2 to 3 hours to set completely before serving.

Nutrition Info:
- 347 calories; 9 g protein; 16 g total fat; 8 g saturated fat; 39 g carbohydrates; 1 g fiber; 271 mg sodium

Coconut Rice Pudding

Servings:6 | Cooking Time:x

Ingredients:

- ¾ cup (165 g) superfine sugar
- 3 cups (750 ml) milk, lactose-free milk, or suitable plant-based milk (more if needed)
- One 13.5-ounce (400 ml) can light coconut milk
- 2 teaspoons vanilla extract
- 1½ cups (300 g) Arborio rice
- Heaping ¼ cup (20 g) shredded sweetened or unsweetened coconut
- Maple syrup, for serving (optional)

Directions:

1. Combine the sugar, milk, coconut milk, and vanilla in a medium saucepan over medium-high heat and bring to a boil, stirring regularly. Add the rice. Reduce the heat and simmer, stirring regularly, for about 50 minutes, until the liquid has been absorbed and the rice is tender. Add extra milk if required.

2. Meanwhile, preheat the oven to 325°F (170°C) and line a baking sheet with foil. Sprinkle the coconut over the baking sheet and bake for 10 to 12 minutes, until it is just starting to turn golden brown.

3. Serve the rice pudding warm or at room temperature, topped with the toasted coconut and a drizzle of maple syrup, if desired.

Nutrition Info:

- 417 calories; 9 g protein; 7 g total fat; 5 g saturated fat; 78 g carbohydrates; 1 g fiber; 85 mg sodium

Irish Cream Delights

Servings:6 | Cooking Time:x

Ingredients:

- ½ cup (125 ml) light cream
- ½ cup (110 g) packed light brown sugar
- 2 cups (500 ml) milk, lactose-free milk, or suitable plant-based milk
- ½ cup (125 ml) Irish cream liqueur, such as Baileys
- ¼ cup (35 g) cornstarch
- Shaved chocolate, for serving

Directions:

1. Combine the cream, brown sugar, and 1¾ cup (435 ml) of the milk in a medium saucepan and cook over medium heat until almost boiling. Stir in the liqueur.

2. Blend the cornstarch with the remaining ¼ cup (60 ml) of milk to form a smooth paste. Gradually add to the warm cream mixture, stirring constantly to ensure there are no lumps, then cook, stirring, over medium heat for about 5 minutes, until thickened. (Don't let it boil.)

3. Pour the pudding into six 4-ounce (125 ml) ramekins. Allow to cool, then cover with plastic wrap and refrigerate for 3 to 4 hours, until set.

4. Decorate with the shaved chocolate just before serving.

Nutrition Info:

- 230 calories; 4 g protein; 8 g total fat; 5 g saturated fat; 32 g carbohydrates; 0 g fiber; 76 mg sodium

The Balanced Low-FODMAP Diet Cookbook for Beginners

Rich White Chocolate Cake

Servings:12 | Cooking Time:x

Ingredients:

- Nonstick cooking spray
- 15 tablespoons (2 sticks minus 1 tablespoon/225 g) unsalted butter, cut into cubes
- 7 ounces (200 g) good-quality white chocolate, broken into pieces
- 2¼ cups (475 g) packed light brown sugar
- ¾ cup (65 g) soy flour
- ¾ cup (95 g) tapioca flour
- 1 cup (130 g) superfine white rice flour
- ½ cup (75 g) cornstarch
- 2 teaspoons xanthan gum or guar gum
- 1 teaspoon baking soda
- 1 teaspoon gluten-free baking powder
- 2 teaspoons vanilla extract
- 2 large eggs
- Confectioners' sugar, for dusting

Directions:

1. Preheat the oven to 300°F (150°C). Grease a 9-inch (23 cm) springform pan with cooking spray.
2. Combine the butter, white chocolate, brown sugar, and 1½ cups (375 ml) hot water in a medium heatproof bowl or the top part of a double boiler. Set over a saucepan of simmering water or the bottom part of the double boiler (make sure the bottom of the bowl does not touch the water) and stir until the chocolate and butter are melted and everything is well combined. Set aside to cool to room temperature.
3. Sift the soy flour, tapioca flour, rice flour, cornstarch, xanthan gum, baking soda, and baking powder three times into a medium bowl (or whisk in the bowl until well combined). Add the cooled white chocolate mixture, vanilla, and eggs and beat with a handheld electric mixer until smooth.
4. Pour the batter into the pan and bake for 45 minutes. Cover with foil and bake for 15 to 30 minutes more, until firm to the touch (a toothpick inserted into the center should come out clean).
5. Cool in the pan for 15 minutes, then remove the outer ring and turn out onto a wire rack to cool completely. Dust with confectioners' sugar before serving.

Nutrition Info:

- 496 calories; 7 g protein; 21 g total fat; 13 g saturated fat; 73 g carbohydrates; 1 g fiber; 196 mg sodium

Carrot Parsnip Chips

Servings:3 | Cooking Time: 35 Minutes

Ingredients:

- 1 large parsnip, peeled and ends cut off
- 1 large carrot, peeled and ends cut off
- 2 tsp olive oil
- Pinch of salt
- 1 tsp thyme leaves

Directions:

1. Preheat the oven to 325°F.
2. Oil a baking tray lightly.
3. Peel the carrot and parsnip into long thin pieces and place onto the tray. Drizzle with oil and season.
4. Cook for 35 minutes, turning the vegetables 2 times during cooking.

Nutrition Info:

- 386g Calories, 10g Total fat, 1g Saturated fat, 73g Carbohydrates, 20 g Fiber, 6g Protein, 24g Sodium

Flourless Chocolate Cake

Servings:8 | Cooking Time:x

Ingredients:

- Nonstick cooking spray
- ⅓ cup (35 g) unsweetened cocoa powder, plus more for dusting
- 10 tablespoons (1¼ sticks/150 g) unsalted butter, cut into cubes, at room temperature
- 5 ounces (150 g) good-quality dark chocolate, broken into pieces
- 1¼ cups (275 g) packed light brown sugar
- 1¼ cups (150 g) almond flour
- 4 large eggs, separated
- Gluten-free, lactose-free ice cream, for serving (optional)

Directions:

1. Preheat the oven to 300°F (150°C). Grease a 9-inch (23 cm) springform pan with cooking spray and line with a parchment paper circle.
2. Combine the cocoa, butter, dark chocolate, and ⅓ cup (80 ml) water in a medium saucepan over low heat and stir until melted and smooth. Remove from the heat and stir in the brown sugar, almond flour, and egg yolks. Transfer to a large bowl and let cool to room temperature.
3. Beat the egg whites in a clean bowl with a handheld electric mixer until soft peaks form. Gently fold the egg whites into the cooled chocolate mixture in two batches.
4. Pour the batter into the prepared springform pan and bake for 55 to 65 minutes, until firm when pressed gently in the center.
5. Cool in the pan for 20 minutes, then remove the outer ring and turn out onto a wire rack to cool completely. Dust with additional cocoa and serve with ice cream, if desired.

Nutrition Info:

- 398 calories; 7 g protein; 26 g total fat; 12 g saturated fat; 40 g carbohydrates; 4 g fiber; 44 mg sodium

Chinese Chicken In Lettuce Cups

Servings:4 | Cooking Time: 5 Minutes

Ingredients:

- 2 tablespoons gluten-free soy sauce
- 2 tablespoons rice vinegar
- ½ teaspoon salt
- ½ teaspoon sugar
- 2 tablespoons vegetable oil
- 2 teaspoons Garlic Oil (here)
- 2 teaspoons minced fresh ginger
- 1 pound boneless, skinless chicken breasts, minced
- ½ cup water chestnuts, minced
- 8 to 10 inner leaves iceberg lettuce, edges trimmed and chilled
- Handful of fresh cilantro leaves, coarsely chopped
- ¼ cup unsalted roasted peanuts, coarsely chopped (optional)

Directions:

1. In a small bowl, stir together the soy sauce, rice vinegar, salt, and sugar.
2. Heat the vegetable oil and Garlic Oil in a skillet or wok set over high heat. Add the ginger and cook, stirring, for 10 seconds. Add the chicken and cook, stirring, for about 1 minute, until the chicken is opaque all over. Add the water chestnuts and reduce to medium-low. Stir in the soy sauce mixture and cook for about 2 minutes more, until the chicken is cooked through.
3. Arrange the lettuce cups on a platter or serving plates and spoon some of the chicken mixture into each, dividing equally. Garnish each serving with cilantro and peanuts, if using, and serve immediately.

Nutrition Info:

- Calories: 378; Protein: 36g; Total Fat: 19g; Saturated Fat: 4g; Carbohydrates: 14g; Fiber: 1g; Sodium: 778mg;

Macadamia–chocolate Chip Cookies

Servings:x | Cooking Time:x

Ingredients:
- MAKES 20
- 8 tablespoons (1 stick/120 g) unsalted butter, cut into cubes, at room temperature
- ¼ cup (55 g) packed light brown sugar
- ¼ cup (55 g) superfine sugar
- 1 large egg
- 1 teaspoon vanilla extract
- ⅔ cup (85 g) superfine white rice flour
- ½ cup (75 g) cornstarch
- ¼ cup (20 g) soy flour
- ½ teaspoon baking soda
- ½ cup (95 g) chocolate chips
- ½ cup (70 g) roasted unsalted macadamia nuts, roughly chopped

Directions:
1. Preheat the oven to 325°F (170°C). Line two baking sheets with parchment paper.
2. Combine the butter, brown sugar, and superfine sugar in a medium bowl and beat with a handheld electric mixer until thick and pale. Add the egg and vanilla and beat well.
3. Sift the rice flour, cornstarch, soy flour, and baking soda three times into a bowl (or whisk in the bowl until well combined). Add to the butter mixture and beat well, then stir in the chocolate chips and macadamia nuts.
4. Drop tablespoons of dough onto the sheets, leaving room for spreading. Bake for 10 to 15 minutes, until golden. Cool on the sheets for 5 minutes, then transfer to a wire rack to cool completely.

Nutrition Info:
- 142 calories; 2 g protein; 9 g total fat; 4 g saturated fat; 16 g carbohydrates; 1 g fiber; 37 mg sodium

Baked Blueberry Cheesecakes

Servings:9 | Cooking Time:x

Ingredients:
- 7 ounces (250 g) gluten-free vanilla cookies, crushed (about 2 cups)
- 4 tablespoons (½ stick/60 g) unsalted butter, melted
- 2 cups (300 g) fresh or frozen blueberries
- Two 8-ounce (225 g) packages reduced-fat cream cheese, at room temperature
- One 14-ounce (396 g) can fat-free sweetened condensed milk
- 2 teaspoons vanilla extract
- ½ cup (125 ml) light whipping cream
- 2 large eggs
- ¼ cup (35 g) cornstarch

Directions:
1. Preheat the oven to 325°F (160°C).
2. Mix together the crushed cookies and melted butter, then press into the bottom of nine 4-inch (10 cm) springform pans. Divide the blueberries evenly over the cookie crusts.
3. Combine the cream cheese, condensed milk, vanilla, cream, eggs, and cornstarch in a food processor or blender and process until smooth. Pour the batter over the crusts. Bake for 15 to 20 minutes, until lightly golden and firm to the touch.
4. Allow to cool completely in the pans, then cover and refrigerate for 3 hours before serving.

Nutrition Info:
- 512 calories; 9 g protein; 18 g total fat; 9 g saturated fat; 37 g carbohydrates; 1 g fiber; 252 mg sodium

Appendix : Recipes Index

A

Acorn Squash And Chard Soup 62

Amaretti Tiramisu 88

Arroz Con Pollo With Olives, Raisins, And Pine Nuts 34

Artisanal Ketchup 76

Atlantic Cod With Basil Walnut Sauce 19

Autumn Breakfast Chia Bowl 7

B

Bacon Mashed Potatoes 68

Baked Blueberry Cheesecakes 93

Baked Moroccan-style Halibut 25

Baked Tofu And Vegetables 45

Baked Veggie Chips 82

Basic Baked Scallops 25

Basic Marinara Sauce 78

Basic Smoothie Base 4

Basil Sauce 75

Beef Rolls With Horseradish Cream 40

Blueberry, Kiwi, And Mint 11

Bolognese Sauce 72

Breakfast Ratatouille With Poached Eggs 6

Butter Lettuce Salad With Poached Egg And Bacon 61

C

Caesar Salad Dressing 79

Caprese Salad 67

Carrot Parsnip Chips 91

Cheese And Herb Scones 4

Cheese Strata 52

Cheese, Ham, And Spinach Muffins 9

Chia Seed Carrot Cake Pudding 9

Chicken And Dumplings Soup 69

Chicken And Rice With Peanut Sauce 30

Chicken Liver Paté With Pepper And Sage 2

Chicken Noodle Soup 58

Chicken Noodle Soup With Bok Choy 65

Chinese Chicken 41

Chinese Chicken In Lettuce Cups 92

Chipotle Tofu And Sweet Potato Tacos With Avocado Salsa 51

Chocolate Lava Cakes 83

Chocolate Scones 12

Chopped Italian Salad 63

Cilantro-coconut Pesto 76

Cinnamon Panna Cotta With Pureed Banana 85

Citrus Fennel And Mint Salad 59

Citrusy Swordfish Skewers 15

Coconut Rice Pudding 90

Coconut Shrimp 16

Coconut-crusted Fish With Pineapple Relish 17

Coconut-curry Tofu With Vegetables 45

Collard Green Wraps With Thai Peanut Dressing 49

Cornmeal-crusted Tilapia 24

Cranberry Almond Granola 5

Cranberry Chocolate Chip Energy Bites 8

Cranberry Orange Scones 10

Crêpes With Cheese Sauce 3

Crustless Spinach Quiche 48

Cucumber And Sesame Salad 67

Cucumbers With Cottage Cheese Ranch Dip 88

Cumin Turkey With Fennel 37

D

Dairy-free Coffee Ice Cream 89

Deviled Eggs 86

E

Easy Onion- And Garlic-free Chicken Stock 64

Eggs Baked In Heirloom Tomatoes 10

F

Feta Crab Cakes 24

Fish And Chips 17

Fish And Potato Pie 32

Flanken-style Beef Ribs With Quick Slaw 29

Flourless Chocolate Cake 92

Flourless Vegan Banana Peanut Butter Pancakes 11

G

Garden Pesto 79

Garden Veggie Dip Burgers 32

Garlic Oil 77
Garlic-infused Oil 75
Ginger Sesame Salad Dressing 73
Ginger-sesame Grilled Flank Steak 29
Glorious Strawberry Salad 61
Greek Pasta Salad 58
Grilled Cod With Fresh Basil 16
Grilled Halibut With Lemony Pesto 27

H

Hawaiian Toasted Sandwich 8
Homemade Barbecue Sauce 72
Huevos Rancheros 13

I

Irish Cream Delights 90

K

Kale And Red Bell Pepper Salad 66
Kiwi Yogurt Freezer Bars 87

L

Lamb And Vegetable Pilaf 30
Lamb Meatballs 82
Latin Quinoa-stuffed Peppers 50
Layered Tahitian Lime Cheesecake 89
Lemon Cheesecake 81
Lemon Tartlets 85
Lemon Thyme Chicken 34
Lentil Chili 68
Lentil-walnut Burgers 51
Light Tuna Casserole 15
Low-fodmap Hummus 83
Low-fodmap Mayonnaise 74
Low-fodmap Spicy Ketchup 74

M

Mac 'n' Cheeze 52
Macadamia–chocolate Chip Cookies 93
Maple Mustard Dipping Sauce 78
Maple-glazed Salmon 18
Mediterranean Flaky Fish With Vegetables 27
Mediterranean Noodles 43
Mexican Risotto 44

Mexican-style Ground Beef And Rice 33
Mild Lamb Curry 37
Mixed Grains, Seeds, And Vegetable Bowl 46
Mussels In Chili, Bacon, And Tomato Broth 57

N

No-bake Coconut Cookie Bars 84

O

Olive Tapenade 73
Orange-ginger Salmon 38
Overnight Banana Chocolate Oats 11
Overnight Peanut Butter Pumpkin Spice Oats 5

P

Pasta With Pesto Sauce 47
Pb&j Smoothie 12
Peanut Butter Soba Noodles 50
Pepperonata Sauce 79
Philly Steak Sandwich 63
Pineapple Fried Rice 55
Poached Salmon With Tarragon Sauce 20
Pork Loin Rub 73
Potato And Corn Chowder 59
Potato Pancakes 9
Prosciutto-wrapped Cantaloupe 86
Pumpkin Maple Roast Chicken 41
Pumpkin Seed Dressing 71

Q

Quinoa Muffins 87
Quinoa-stuffed Eggplant Roulades With Feta And Mint 43

R

Raspberry Lemon Chia Seed Jam 78
Raspberry–chia Seed Ice Pops 86
Red Snapper With Sweet Potato Crust And Cilantro-lime Sauce 38
Rice Paper "spring Rolls" With Satay Sauce 64
Rich White Chocolate Cake 91
Rita's Linguine With Clam Sauce 19
Roast Beef Tenderloin With Parmesan Crust 35
Roasted Potato Wedges 60
Roasted Squash And Chestnut Soup 62

Roasted Sweet Potato Salad With Spiced Lamb And Spinach 65
Roasted Tomato Sauce 76
Roasted-veggie Gyros With Tzatziki Sauce 47

S

Salmon Cakes With Fresh Dill Sauce 22
Salmon Noodle Casserole 20
Salmon With Herbs 23
Scrambled Tofu 7
Seafood Risotto 26
Shrimp And Cheese Casserole 23
Shrimp Puttanesca With Linguine 22
Shrimp With Cherry Tomatoes 18
Smoky Corn Chowder With Red Peppers 44
Smoky Sourdough Pizza 36
Smoothie Bowl 8
Sole Meunière 21
Spaghetti And Meat Sauce 36
Spanish Meatloaf With Garlic Mashed Potatoes 33
Spanish Rice 55
Steakhouse Rub 71
Steamed Mussels With Saffron-infused Cream 39
Strawberry Smoothie 6
Strawberry-rhubarb Crisp With Oat-pecan Topping 84
Stuffed Zucchini Boats 48
Summery Fish Stew 21
Sun-dried Tomato Pesto 72
Sun-dried Tomato Spread 77
Sweet Chili Garlic Sauce 71
Sweet-and-sour Sauce 77

T

Tangy Lemon Curd 75
Thai Pumpkin Noodle Soup 2
Tilapia Piccata 26
Tomato, Basil, And Olive Risotto 66
Tropical Smoothie 7
Turkey And Red Pepper Burgers 31
Turkey Bolognese With Pasta 35
Turkey Pasta With Kale 39
Turkey Quinoa Meatballs With Mozzarella 31
Turkey-ginger Soup 57

V

Vegan Carrot, Leek, And Saffron Soup 60
Vegan Noodles With Gingered Coconut Sauce 53
Vegan Pad Thai 49
Vegan Potato Salad, Cypriot-style 46
Vegetable And Rice Noodle Bowl 54
Vegetable Stir-fry 53
Veggie Dip 67

W

Watercress Zucchini Soup 54

Z

Zucchini Lasagna With Meat Sauce 40

Printed in Great Britain
by Amazon

42591541R10064